Allan Square

Allan Square

SHIRLEY MURPHY

Flanker Press Ltd.
St. John's
2009

Library and Archives Canada Cataloguing in Publication

Murphy, Shirley, 1936-
Allan Square / Shirley Murphy.

ISBN 978-1-897317-37-2

1. Murphy, Shirley, 1936-. 2. Allan Square (St. John's, N.L.)--Biography. 3. St. John's (N.L.)--Biography. I. Title.

FC2196.26.M87A3 2009 971.8'104092 C2009-900626-X

PRINTED IN CANADA

FLANKER PRESS
P.O. BOX 2522, STATION C
ST. JOHN'S, NL, CANADA A1C 6K1
TOLL-FREE: 1-866-739-4420
WWW.FLANKERPRESS.COM

13 12 11 10 09 2 3 4 5 6 7 8

Canada Council for the Arts Conseil des Arts du Canada

We acknowledge the financial support of: the Government of Canada through the Book Publishing Industry Development Program (BPIDP) for our publishing activities; the Canada Council for the Arts, which last year invested $20.1 million in writing and publishing throughout Canada; the Government of Newfoundland and Labrador, Department of Tourism, Culture and Recreation.

To my husband, Ron, whose sense of Caribbean rhythm lured me back to the dance.

And to my Mom and Dad, whose music was over too soon.

"Have courage for the great sorrows in life and patience for the small ones; and when you have laboriously accomplished your daily tasks, go to sleep in peace. God is awake."

Victor Hugo

Preface

There is one sure thing that can be said about Newfoundland: it is unforgettable. Anyone born there remains a Newfoundlander, first and foremost.

It's said that Newfoundlanders are always easy to spot in Heaven. They're the ones who keep nagging God to let them go back home. Who could blame those disconnected spirits for wanting to go back home? Where else will they find a stranger who feels like family? Where else will they find a stranger who often turns out to *be* family? It's a fairly shallow gene pool in Newfoundland and Labrador.

Sometimes entire families wound up leaving lives in Europe, and heading across a treacherous ocean to a place where the only life thriving was in the waters teeming with fish. Settlement was not allowed on the Island way back in the early days. The fishermen gave their labour and made merchants richer. Some intrepid souls literally "took to the hills" and began new lives in a hard new land. Some were rooted out and punished, some kept right on clinging to the rocks.

My mother's people started their new lives in Red Rock, Bonavista Bay. It was not a far cry from poverty-stricken lives in Ireland to poverty-stricken lives clinging to the rocks of Newfoundland.

My father's family also came from Ireland. They went to St. John's and clung to those rocks until they packed up lock, stock and barrel and moved to New York in the 1920s. My father went with them but came back to Newfoundland where he met my mother. He boarded the boat again, intending to go back to his family, when he suddenly decided he really didn't want to leave my mother. He jumped from the boat to the dock, and here we all are!

He never saw his family again.

So my parents began their married life in the Dirty Thirties, the age of the Great Depression.

Newfoundland society before Confederation was one of the "haves" and "have nots." The Depression was almost an equalizing force, in that it slightly narrowed the gulf between the two levels of society.

Everywhere there were great needs evident. Poverty was rampant all over the world, and the great Island in the Atlantic was no different.

Before Confederation with Canada in 1949, there was no social safety net available. The dole, at not even ten cents a day, is almost laughable, but there was nothing funny about it at the time. It was all some souls had to help them survive.

Hard lives make for a hard people, people who can survive a sojourn in a coal pound and come out of it still able to laugh at the rats and the darkness.

My parents were very good people, good people living in bad times. As my mother used to say when coming out of a particularly rough day, week, month or year:

"Live hard, die hard, and go to hell after all!"

Introduction

I awoke with an indefinable sense of sadness and loss. I felt the hot urine as it poured freely from my body into my mother's bed. It ran from a dream in which I was using the toilet.

At the same time a loud banging began at our front door.

My mother jumped up in the bed and began to scream. At first I didn't know if the screaming was because she was scared of the knocking or if she was angry because she was soaking wet – again.

I figured I was in for it.

Then I heard her frantic words as she ran toward the front door.

"Jesus, Mary and Joseph! Lew is dead!" My heart was racing so loud and so fast that it threatened to overpower the continued banging at the front door.

"Lew" was my father. I was seven years old, it was September 1944, and he was dead. I lay in the wet spot all night, willing it to dry and waiting for my mother to come back from the St. John's General Hospital, or as she called it, "the slaughter house."

Two of my mother's girlfriends had been staying with us during Dad's illness. They slept in my parents' double bed with Mom. My spot was at the foot of the bed, and I helplessly peed in it just about every night. I'm sure I must have drowned every flea that made an attempt to infest that bed.

The next morning, very early, I stood in the kitchen and stared out the length of the hall. I saw my mother standing there in her white coat. Her face was weary and etched with sadness. There was a man with her. He was wearing a black suit with a white priest's collar.

He said to her, "Will you tell them, or will I?"

Nobody had to tell me. Sometime later, in the kitchen, I saw my mother sitting in her rocking chair. My four brothers were crying and clinging to her. She looked up and our eyes met.

I turned and walked back into the bedroom, alone with my grief.

That day the house reeked with the chemical smell of black shoe dye. My mother dyed her white shoes black, and she dyed the white ones that I had used that June for my First Communion.

During the three days my father lay waking in our front room on Allan Square, my mother comforted me freely. Every time I broke down it was in her arms. I was sent to stay overnight with cousins, to spare me the show of grief that was going on in our place.

When I was growing up, I never again felt my mother's love as I had during the time my father's body lay in our front room in its grey casket, waiting to be put into the ground.

Chapter 1

The sounds of downtown St. John's were very distinctive in the years I lived there. Among them were the whistle of the train as it neared the station, the peals of the church bells from the big Cathedral of St. John the Baptist, and the Angelus bells, which rang every day at noon. The drone of the foghorns was as steady and predictable as the overcast skies.

I was not actually born on Allan Square. My birthplace was a little ramshackle house in the west end of Livingstone Street, just around the corner from Allan Square.

I was born at home on the twenty-third of December, 1936, helped into the world by a very capable and professional midwife named Mrs. Mullins, a neighbour of my mother's. She was a fine, strapping woman who needed all her strength the night I was born. I presented bum first and she brought my mother and me through that very difficult breech birth with great competence. She was not, however, able to do anything about my appearance. My mother told me I looked exactly like a slimy skinned rabbit when I was born. It must have been a disappointment for her, a first and, as it would turn out, only daughter who looked as if she had just been skinned alive!

I was the fourth child. My three brothers, Jerry, Lew and Jack, were mere babies when I barged my bum into the world. The oldest was only five. Later there was another brother, Bob. My mother must have had it mighty hard that Christmas. From what I've been able to learn, there wasn't much cheer to spread around. She had lost a lot of blood, there were three young boys to look after, and along came another squalling brat to feed. Times were tough in old St. John's, and they were especially tough on Livingstone Street.

Within a year of my birth, we took over the ground floor flat of number eight Allan Square.

As it would turn out, Allan Square was no more of a picnic than Livingstone Street. As a matter of fact, number eight was a bloody cold place. Our family lived on the first floor of the house, which was owned by an absentee landlord who had moved away in search of finer things, to the Boston States.

The rent of ten dollars a month was collected by a St. John's lawyer whose offices were on Duckworth Street next to the courthouse. When I got big enough, I used to trot down there to deliver the ten dollars in cash. By God! They should have paid us to live there, instead of the other way around.

No maintenance was ever done, to the best of my memory, not even a coat of paint for the front. The house was no colour at all, not grey, not black, just an indefinite mottled shade brought about by its standing into the wind for years in all kinds of weather.

You took your life and limbs in your hands climbing the four irregular steps leading up to the front door of the house, but climb them we did, and fall down them I did when I was about three, breaking my collarbone in the process, and landing for an overnight visit in St. Clare's Mercy Hospital, where a crooked-ass bitch of a nurse called me down to the dirt the next morning for wetting the bed. She is my earliest memory of life on Allan Square.

But I must say, St. Clare's Hospital was a lovely, warm place, temperature-wise. Allan Square was cold enough to freeze your ass off. Even at three I took my comfort wherever and whenever I found it. St. Clare's was nice and warm, but the collarbone hurt like hell.

Allan Square is nestled in the shadow of the Roman Catholic Basilica, but the church was not given that status until years later. When we were growing up, it loomed over us as the Cathedral of St. John the Baptist, and in my eyes it was a haven for those who wore black, such as nuns, priests, widows and widowers.

On the east side of Long's Hill was St. Andrew's Presbyterian Church. We simply knew it as the Kirk, which is a Scottish name for "Church." We played our kissing games in the grounds of the Kirk. Down on Church Hill, only a few steps away, was the Anglican Cathedral. Churches, schools, and more churches wherever you looked. I didn't know it then, but I actually grew up surrounded by money. No wonder my mother called me Madam!

Our living area was on the ground floor of the house and consisted of the kitchen, two bedrooms, the front room and the "Lobby," which held the only sink.

The lobby was also home to the infamous coal pound where, of course, the coal was stored. Why it was called the pound I will never know. I also have no idea why the lobby was given that name. The place sure was no hotel. We had no hot water and no bathtub. The bathroom was a dark little room off the hall with a toilet. I don't remember it ever having a light, or a toilet seat. Actually, I didn't find out about toilet seats until I went to school. I guess it's true that what you don't have you don't miss. I do remember having a cold bum on a pretty regular basis.

Still, although the toilet in the hall was damned cold, at least it wasn't an outhouse. We also had "piss-pots" in the bedrooms; they helped on a cold, frosty night.

The only heat in our place was from the big Ideal coal range in the kitchen. In the nights we sat in front of it, basking in its rosy glow until we scampered to the freezing bedrooms, battened down with blankets and whatever coats we could dig up. I was the only girl in a family with four boys, and while my father was alive I slept on a daybed in my parents' bedroom. Not much fun for them, I'm sure, but they had to put me somewhere. God love them.

Bob, the youngest, slept in a crib along one wall in my parents' room, and we both wet our beds on a regular basis.

We sang ourselves to sleep every night and woke up drenched with urine in the mornings. The other three boys slept in a big bed in the remaining bedroom and fought and kicked each other to sleep as part of their nightly routine.

The front room was exactly that; it looked out on Allan Square from its two long, narrow windows. They were covered with lace curtains, which my mother managed to bring new life to with regular rinses of Dolly Dye. The dye was contained in a mysterious, bell-shaped material, which was enclosed in white cloth. It turned the lace curtains to a sickly but clean yellow. If you wanted them really, really yellow, they were simply dipped longer. Tricky process.

The yellow lace curtains are not what I remember most about the front room, though. It's the wallpaper. Oppressive navy blue velvet scrolls of all shapes and sizes wandered haphazardly up and down the walls no matter where the eyes landed. The scrolls always scared me, but they became literally ominous when my father's grey coffin was placed between the two long windows.

The last time I remember seeing my father alive outside our house, he was walking down a steep flight of steps from Harvey Road to Long's Hill, with his checkerboard under his arm. He was a master checkers player. All the kids had learned how to play, but try as we might, we could never beat him.

I found out later that he had just come by bus from the General Hospital, after being told they could do no more for him. He had been diagnosed with an inoperable growth in his throat.

I often think of how worried he must have been, with no one to pick him up from the hospital and the knowledge of his imminent death filling his mind on the bus ride home. He could not talk, but he smiled at me and held out his hand. I grabbed his thumb, felt its pulse and warmth and was contented. I revelled in the sunshine, holding onto that thumb for dear life, skipping beside my father down Long's Hill to Allan Square.

Mom didn't let me come into the house with him. The door closed and I was left on the steps. I was very upset about it then, but now I realize they had a lot of serious problems to deal with that day, and they didn't need a seven-year-old girl to share their worries.

Before my father's death Allan Square was a happy place, as far as I was concerned. There were often relatives visiting and people with musical instruments. My uncle Pete, from St. Mary's Bay, always visited our place when he came into town, which, granted, wasn't often. I still remember his nimble fingers dancing over thc accordion keys and his tap dancing shaking the kitchen floor. He had the happiest brown eyes I have ever seen. There was also a man who played the spoons, and his performances absolutely delighted me. There were singers coming out of the woodwork, and good ones at that. Everyone sat around in a circle and each stood to take a turn belting out a song, mostly ballads, some obscure, others familiar.

When the time came for the visitors to go "beddy bye-bye," kitchen chairs were used to make beds. No doubt bad backs abounded, but the welcome was warm.

Every Sunday before his death, I went to Mass with my father. We always stayed out in the vestibule leading into the main church. The entrance doors were open, so that those on the outside could hear the sermon and the Latin service.

The outer lobby of the church was entirely filled with men, each of them down on one knee; my father was always among them. These men were called the "gunners," a carry-over from the days when it was forbidden in Newfoundland to practice the Catholic faith. The gunners had, historically, watched the back of the church to ensure that no law enforcement agents could creep up on practitioners of the Catholic faith.

I stood encircled by my father's arm as he knelt on one knee, and I watched with interest the sea of legs and shoes, the only things in my line of vision. During a certain part of the Mass, men struggled to make their way among us, holding out baskets. My father dug into his pocket and passed me a few coins to toss into the basket. This, I later learned, was called the collection.

My dad also took me visiting after Mass on Sundays. He was a very sociable person and kept in touch with his few relatives who remained in St. John's.

I don't think my father's mother ever really forgave him for coming back to Newfoundland. She certainly didn't write to him. If it was not for the letters his sister sent, we would never have known that we had relatives in the States. After my father died we also lost touch with the few relatives remaining in St. John's.

My father obviously did not forget his sojourn in the States. Every weekend he sent one of my brothers to a store on Duckworth Street to buy the New York and Boston papers.

My father's uncle, James, was the first male of the family to leave St. John's. He moved to Boston, and his later claim to fame was becoming the father of journalist and biographer Charles J. V. Murphy, who had a list of literary credits to his name that could have choked a horse, including ghostwriting *The Heart Has Its Reasons* by the Duchess of Windsor and co-writing *The Windsor Story* with J. Bryan III. Murphy was commissioned by *Life* magazine to write the memoirs of King Edward VIII. This went on to become the highly successful *A King's Story.* He also wrote and co-wrote a number of biographies of luminaries who happened to be floating in his particular orbit, including Winston Churchill. Unfortunately, Murphy became alienated from his father, James, and the other members of his father's second family. They were never to meet again as a family in this life.

Murphy accompanied Admiral Byrd to the South Pole in 1934, serving as a communications officer for the Byrd Antarctic Expedition. He broadcast to CBS regularly and contributed articles on the expedition to the *Boston Globe*.

My great-grandfather, Philip Murphy, worked at Bowring Brothers as a tally master and lived at 114 George Street. He was a lifelong member of the Total Abstinence Society, or the TA as it was called. I often wonder what he would think of George Street now. His poor sober soul is probably reeling in horror against the walls of one of the many establishments lining both sides of that pub-famous street.

Although Philip Murphy fathered thirteen children with my great-grandmother Bridget Hearn, when he passed away he was survived by only three sons, Nicholas in St. John's, James in Boston, and my grandfather Lewis, also in St. John's. Philip certainly suffered a great deal of loss in his life.

All of which goes to shed a little light on why we grew up with no Murphy relatives in St. John's. After my father's death, the ones we did have seemed to have no knowledge of, or interest in, our existence.

One of Dad's relatives we visited, while Dad was still with us, lived in what was then the outskirts of St. John's, Oxen Pond Road. Her name was Kitty Gover, and we visited her frequently and were given bully-beef sandwiches and tea. During the Second World War, her son, who was in the RAF, was shot down by the Germans over France. Our house was locked in grief; everyone was in tears. I knew my father and mother must have felt very close to that young man.

We had one gas mask in our house, and we had ration books. Every evening the news was filled with action stories from the Front. There was a radio report about the Red Army slowly making its steady way across Europe toward Berlin.

I had a picture in my mind of a large horde of red men in battledress. I figured they might be capable of getting to where we were. I didn't know if they were friends or foes, but I do remember the reports scared the living shit out of me.

We also had blackouts, where no lights were supposed to show from any window in any house. We had men who were blackout wardens patrolling the streets and checking for unlawful lights. There could be no lights showing anywhere at all, and the nights were black as pitch. That was so the enemy flyers, if they ventured across the Atlantic, would not be able to identify inhabited areas and bomb them.

My father worked as a night watchman in Baird's Cove, and I constantly worried the German U-Boats would sneak into St. John's Harbour and take him away. But he always came home safely in the morning. Sometimes he brought fresh coconuts and real pineapples. Exotic fruits were a novelty in our house and in just about every other house in the area.

I remember hearing at the time – as I managed to hear everything that went on in our house – that Hitler had said he would "Drop a loaf of bread on Newfoundland," and that would be enough to finish it off. Didn't he know we had the American bases to protect us and the rest of North America?

On the night of December 12, 1942, I was asleep on my cot in my parents' bedroom when I was suddenly snapped awake by the sound of loud voices coming from the kitchen.

The adults were listening to the *Barn Dance,* a musical show that was broadcast by VOCM radio from the Knights of Columbus Hostel on Harvey Road. The sky outside my bedroom window was blood red. I couldn't figure out what had happened. I thought that we had been bombed and the whole city was on fire. I heard the next day there had been a tremendous loss of life in a fire at the Knights of Columbus Hostel, which was frequented by large numbers of the military.

The next morning I made my way up to Harvey Road to see for myself the disastrous, black remains of the fire. I don't know how I got out of the house, but I did. The scene was under military guard, but nobody seemed to notice me.

The red sky I saw when I woke was burned into my memory. Anything else I know about the fire I have since read. Medical aid and supplies flooded in from Boston to St. John's. Shortly afterward there were fires in Boston at the Coconut Grove and in Halifax. The spots were all places frequented by members of the armed forces.

There was talk about espionage.

Chapter 2

After my father's death, my mother came up with some very inventive ways of making ends meet to put a bit of grub on the table.

The three female boarders she had living with us were out-of-town friends of hers and they paid a weekly board. Two of them were actually living with us when my Dad passed away. It was wartime and everything was rationed. Some things, like nylons, were simply unavailable.

I remember the girls putting makeup on their legs and drawing a black seam up the back with some sort of marker. I wondered how that was going to keep their legs warm.

To put it mildly, they did liven the place up considerably.

I have no idea how in God's name we fit them all into the ground floor flat of Allan Square, but fit them in we did.

There was no shortage of men in town, even though most of the locals were away in the forces. The Yanks from the nearby American base of Fort Pepperrell were hated by the men of St. John's and adored by most of the ladies.

My brothers probably got a big kick out of having the girls living with us. There was always a fair bit of flesh showing in the kitchen as they prepared for their dates, and the radio was constantly tuned to the American Forces station VOUS, Voice of the United States.

The girls pranced around in their slips and bras. They sang along with the music while shampooing their hair and applying makeup. I didn't have a bra – didn't need one – or I might have joined in their fun.

I wasn't that happy about our female boarders, because when Dad was in the hospital, I had to sleep in my parents' bed sandwiched between Mom and one of the two boarders. My head rested at the foot of the bed because neither Mom nor the boarder wanted to get soaked during the night. There was nowhere to put my feet, except toward the head of the bed. This meant that when I peed on my mother during the night I also christened the boarder, as I rubbed my feet into her sleeping face. The other girl slept like a dry, comfy baby in my poor old daybed.

One evening, as we were listening to the Bob Hope show on VOUS, the girls' routines began to vary a bit. Just as Bob was opening with his theme song, *It Pays To Be Ignorant,* I watched with interest as the girls began to scratch their heads and whisper among themselves. I didn't think much about the scratching part, because my own head was constantly itchy.

The next thing I knew, one of the girls drenched her hair under the cold-water tap. She then spread a newspaper on the kitchen table and searched in her purse, finally pulling out a fine-tooth comb.

Next, a big aluminum pan was dragged from somewhere, filled with water, and placed on the table on top of the paper.

The first boarder spread her legs, leaned over the table, and put her head directly over the pan. As she began to vigorously pull the comb through her dyed-blonde locks, I watched in fascination as what looked like hundreds of little black creatures tumbled unceremoniously into the pan. She had a look of distaste on her face, and combed until her head must have been raw and all the lice drowned, or died from brain damage after hitting the sides of the pan.

She obviously didn't know that a fine-tooth comb would not get rid of the nits.

In turn, each of the girls performed the same task. Strangely enough, they all had their own fine-tooth combs. This was obviously a recurring problem. I had never seen the demise of lice all at once before, so it was new to me.

Mom had a weary look on her face, as if she knew her boarders would soon be leaving. Nobody could blame them. After all, they were each trying to snag a Yank, and a lousy girlfriend was *persona non grata* to any American serviceman and their fastidious superiors.

The only thing that would have been worse than a lousy girlfriend to a Yank would have been one who had a sexually transmitted disease.

Anyway, as my mother suspected would happen, the girls left. They hated to leave my mother on her own, but they did it gently. They left a week at a time, first one, then the others, until finally there was no more dancing in the kitchen.

The girls were completely deloused by the time they left, thanks to a foul-smelling brew that was available at the corner drugstore, guaranteed to kill any louse that had a leg left to stand on.

It was also guaranteed to blow their eggs, the infamous nits, into oblivion.

The girls left with regret, but they were much happier. Not a one of them scratched even once as they kissed us goodbye and sailed out the door with their suitcases. We still listened to VOUS after the girls left.

Now our small family was free to starve quietly and to scratch ourselves to death, until we could scrounge up enough cash to get some of the deadly brew that promised to banish the lice forever. The drugstore didn't give credit.

It wasn't too long after the boarders moved on to other quarters that Mom hatched a promising plan to bring a little money into our house.

After Dad's death the front room served for a while as a bedroom. Then with an eye toward making a desperately needed buck, Mom made the front room "off limits" to all the kids and got it ready for renting. She moved the boys back into the small bedroom where they had slept before Dad's death. My youngest brother, Bob, was moved to a crib in her room, and I went back in the daybed, which she placed along the wall on one side of her bedroom. Right under the window, which provided hearty blasts of cold air on a regular basis. I had nobody to pee on except myself.

She then turned her attention to the front room. It was empty and that meant it could be rented out to anyone who was foolish enough to tackle it.

A milliner named Miss Moore was the lucky tenant. A small coal stove was found for the room so that she wouldn't freeze to death and could boil a drop of water for a cup of tea, and we were soon in business. I have absolutely no memory of how or if the poor woman cooked a meal. It must have been something like going out in the country for a boil-up. Or maybe she lived on cold beans.

I do know that she had a romantic interest in her life. A member of the Canadian Forces visited her regularly. Maybe he brought food, too.

He was tall and handsome and looked dashing in his uniform. He took a liking to me, and often we walked together to a little shop at the end of Theatre Hill where they sold ice cream.

We would walk quietly back up the hill. Revelling in his company, I always took great pleasure – and time – in disposing of my ice cream. He helped to assuage the loneliness I was feeling for my father.

Miss Moore must also have taken a liking to me, because she presented me with a beautiful bonnet, all ribbons and frills. I loved it and wore it to the annual funeral Mass at Mount Carmel Cemetery. I sat on the grave and talked to Dad.

Miss Moore did not last long enough in the room to make me another bonnet.

One day I was sitting on our front steps when I heard a godawful crash and the breaking of glass. I jumped out of the way just in time to avoid getting hit in the head by the little coal stove from her sitting room.

Somehow or other a fire had started in the front room, and some brave soul, probably her military man, had decided against trying to douse the fire. Instead, the entire stove, chimney pipe and all, was simply tossed through the window. Lucky for me I was a fast mover.

I don't know where Miss Moore slept that night, but I didn't see her again at Allan Square.

When she left she took my favourite military man with her, and there were no more outings down Theatre Hill for ice cream.

That ended Mom's fledging forays into the business of rooming and boarding houses.

We would have to find another way to supplement our food supply.

Chapter 3

"Fly!" my mother screamed at me. "Fly curs-ed to hell's fiery flames! And forget that you ever heard of Allan Square! Evaporate!"

Many a time I ducked my head, just barely avoiding being hit by the damp washrag she aimed my way. I can't remember (coincidence or brain damage?) how many times I feared I'd been rendered stone deaf. In those days there was no such thing as scarring a child through corporal punishment. In fact, the opposite was true. "Spare the rod and spoil the child" was the edict in our house, and also in my school. Whichever way a kid turned, violence and cracks in the head were a daily risk factor. The nuns used the strap for the slightest infringement of school rules.

At home I never did get it with the belt, though. Thank God for small mercies.

"I'll kill you! You slut!" was a popular daily endearment. When I got old enough to read, I looked up "slut" in the dictionary and promptly decided that Mom must have made a mistake. I was a kid; therefore, I definitely didn't meet the requirements for the dictionary's definition of "untidy woman."

When I got older I realized that she had one hell of a life herself, left widowed in pre-Confederation Newfoundland, with five children under thirteen and no social safety net at all. There we were, starving to death quietly in that godforsaken house on Allan Square. We had no help, except from Mom's sister and her husband who shared with us everything they had, God bless them.

We all muddled along for two years, with me spitting on my toast to keep my brothers from devouring it, when suddenly there appeared on the scene a man who was to become the stepfather. Brave or crazy bugger, I still haven't figured out which one he was. A fortune teller had told Mom that she would marry again, a man who worked with cars and who "tipped his elbow."

This fortune teller had a stellar reputation in St. John's, and her readings were reputed to be very accurate; to the letter, in fact.

When Bill did eventually turn up, the new man on the block proved to have been a friend of my father's in his youth. He might have had the urge to rescue us from starvation or the orphanage, both possibilities very close on our horizons. Or he might have had a real passion for my mother. Who knows what evil lurks in the hearts of men? I never did believe in the fictional response "The Shadow knows": there must have been a more carnal reason.

The first memory I have of my stepfather is of the day he moved into the house on Allan Square, as if we weren't crowded enough before his arrival. He brought a larger-than-life personality, a big mouth, a four-foot statue of the Carmelite sister, St. Thérèse, commonly referred to as the "Little Flower," and a lovely dining room suite of dark wood.

The suite consisted of a table, six chairs, a hutch, and a buffet. The buffet, I remember, was filled with factory glass, cups, and saucers and plates in varying pastel shades. I was fascinated. The furniture smelled of new varnish and glistened a rich, dark brown. It was placed in the front room where my father's casket had lain, between the two long windows. It only served to add to my resentment of the new man.

What was he doing, walking around alive, when my father was gone? And living in our poor old shack of a house. Not only that, but he came from the other side of St. John's, for God's sake. At that time in our history, the area was not considered a desirable address at all. But anyway, there he was, large as life and, as I was to soon discover, twice as mean.

In what seemed a very short period of time, the second part of the fortune teller's prediction began to rear its ugly head: the "elbow tipping" part began to manifest, usually on the weekends.

Tip his elbow my new stepfather did, regularly. When he was drunk he had an absolutely astonishing vocabulary. By the time I was ten, I knew every curse word in the books, and a few that never reached print because they were too foul.

I began to savour my new vocabulary. The cursing of my stepfather was enhanced by my mother's colourful turn of phrase. She didn't swear, but she did have a wonderful way with words, and I was becoming quite rounded in my speech. Of course, I never uttered any of the swear words out loud. There I was, at nine or ten, walking around with the worst language of the docks rattling around in my head, like today's kids and rap songs. Lovely.

And I didn't even have a headset. Look, Ma! No brains.

My family called me "Granny," which I loathed. The nickname came about because they thought I was old-fashioned and knew a lot of things about a lot of things. I hated it then and I still hate it. My grandkids all call me Nana; no Granny for me, thank you very much, been there, done that.

In the meantime, my stepfather was gearing up into fine form. Saturday night was his night to howl. He'd stagger in the door, "spavilized" and spoiling for a fight. My mother was a gutsy little creature, and she was always ready, after a certain amount of provocation, to oblige him. Invariably the shit hit the fan about an hour after he made his appearance.

He'd eat his supper, which had been warming in the oven for about three hours, and then all hell would break loose.

There were about three other houses on the street in which the same scenario was playing out at about the same time on a Saturday night.

Part of the reason for this was the fact that Dynamite Dunne's Tavern was just down the street on Theatre Hill.

When the drunks got kicked out of there, they'd wind their way to the only other places where they had some assurance of not getting kicked out right away, and the prospect of a good fight. They also didn't fear winding up with a broken jaw or damage to some more vital part of their anatomy. Their opponents were usually smaller and weaker, whose only weapons were their tongues. My mother's tongue, as I've already mentioned, was formidable and seemed to put a red haze into my stepfather's eyes.

They were married at St. Joseph's Church, which was close to where my mom's sister lived. I suppose they must have had a bit of a reception for a few friends at my aunt's house. I was never privy to the details. Of course, I was only nine or ten years old at the time, and it was probably considered to be none of my business.

My mom had a new outfit for her wedding. She wore a skirt and jacket in a soft cocoa brown over a mustard-coloured blouse with black polka dots, and a scarf of the same material flowing over the lapels of the jacket. The outfit was finished off with dark brown suede shoes and a brown purse.

We had a babysitter for the evening. One of our older cousins was brave enough to take on the job. She really didn't have a clue as to what she was letting herself in for. The boys were barely civilized, and they were drunk with freedom.

As soon as the front door closed behind the soon-to-be newlyweds, the place went up like fireworks. Pillow fights galore were soon under way.

The sitter joined in enthusiastically, but all she got out of it was a crown of feathers on her blonde head. There was no TV, no video games, none of the amusements that are used to keep kids under control nowadays. What else was there but pillows? And they weren't used lightly. They came down on anyone in sight with all the amazing strength and pent-up energy of a pack of boys. I hid away somewhere until the worst of it was over.

When I ventured into the kitchen, there was a new

entertainment under way. One of the boys had spirited a brand new puppy into the house. My brother had his Boy Scout hat in hand – it looked like the hats the Mounties wear – and the pup was placed in it. His soulful, trusting eyes stared up at my brother just before the hat began to twirl and spin. After about fifteen minutes of spinning, I was beginning to feel dizzy myself. The hat was laid on the floor and the poor pup was hauled out and set on his feet. He immediately began to stagger around the room, bumping into chairs, tables and anything else he touched.

The boys, cruel little bastards, got a big kick out of it. As soon as the pup began to get his bearings, he was once more dumped back into the hat, and the whole process began again with the same result. The babysitter finally called a halt when the dog threw up and dropped like a stone. He immediately went to sleep and didn't get up till the next morning.

Lew said to Jerry, "I wonder why we didn't go to the wedding?"

My older brother answered simply. "Because we weren't invited, that's why!"

I think after that the boys played cards. I went to bed, thinking about the dessert everyone was probably eating at my aunt's place. Fat lot of good it did me.

I believe my stepfather slipped back into his bachelor routine shortly after the marriage.

He was probably thinking to himself, "What in the name of sweet Jesus am I after doin'? Where did all them youngsters come from, anyway?"

One night he came home loaded to the gills and must have started to get mouthy. For some reason or other I was in the kitchen, and my brothers were in bed.

At the sound of his raised voice, my oldest brother bolted like a bat out of hell from the bedroom and tackled my stepfather in a bold move that brought him to the floor. With that the other two boys, in their long johns, raced into the kitchen and joined in keeping my stepfather pinned down. It ended peacefully. My stepfather finally struggled to his feet with a bemused look on his face, walked into the bedroom and fell, fully clothed, into bed. His pockets were empty the next morning.

I was proud of my brothers, and I had enjoyed the take-down enormously. The bigger they come, the harder they fall!

Later that same night, there was a frantic knocking on our front door. I ran to answer it and saw one of the neighbouring women. Her eyes were pouring tears and her face was a study in panic and fear. She kept looking around the street as if she was expecting someone at any minute. She was seeking refuge from her husband, who was drunk. I was just opening the door to let her in when a loud bellow came from their house.

He was in a second-floor window, dangling an infant by its ankles.

"Ya whore! If ye wants yer baby ye'll get the fuck back here and fast, ya slut!"

Without a second's hesitation she immediately turned and beat it home, closing the door gently behind her. She didn't have a prayer against him.

Years later, when I saw Michael Jackson dangling the baby from the window of his hotel, I was overpowered by the same sense of revulsion I had felt when looking out my front door that night so long ago.

The terrified neighbour did wind up having her vengeance, though; she outlived him smartly by thirty or so years.

Drinking, one of my wiser friends later told me, was a good man's failing. It certainly was on Allan Square. Never a dull moment. It seemed that a large number of men in St. John's couldn't hold their liquor, and it was a common sight to see them staggering along the street, even during the day-time. Drunken men and wild dogs roamed the streets and disturbed the peace at will. The police did their best, I suppose, but they couldn't arrest a guy for simply staggering; for all they knew he could have some affliction which affected his equilibrium. They could pick the guy up only if he was falling-down drunk or disturbing the peace. The men were cunning: they waited until they got home to begin the hostilities. In the man's castle there was only a helpless woman to deal with, and that they could handle with little or no sweat.

My best friend, Moll, and I often promised each other that when we got older and married a man, if he showed the first sign of aggressive drunken behaviour, we would lay him flat. Better to go down fighting, we decided, and we relished in the thought.

Let's face it. The father figures in our lives were absolute bastards when drunk. My mother often called my stepfather a bastard during their battles.

He always replied, "Don't you call me a bastard, you trollop! I can't be a bastard. I'm my mother's third child!"

Go figure.

My mother always said she would sooner eat scraps with a sober man than steak with a drunken one. Although my stepfather never laid a finger on me, or threatened me in any physical way, my mother didn't have to sell me on that one. I agreed with her.

Trauma is trauma. The damage was done, as far as I was concerned.

I began to suffer from silent anxiety attacks. My heart raced and my knees shook for no apparent reason.

My brother Jack, painfully shy, lived with constant fear. He often said to me, "Something awful is going to happen!"

I don't remember how old they were, but two of my brothers and a couple of neighbourhood boys from Theatre Hill decided they were going to run away.

Nobody had the slightest idea where they had gone, and the police had to be notified. The effect on our household was frightening. My mother was worried stiff, and even my stepfather showed a small degree of what passed for concern. I was sick with fear and knew then how much I loved and needed my brothers. I promised God that I would be good for the rest of my life if He brought them home safely. That was a desperate promise on my part. I was destined to break it many times.

They were eventually located up in cottage country, around Whitbourne, I think. They had broken into a cabin looking for some food for Jack, who was getting weak. The police brought them home in the Black Maria. It pulled in to the Square and backed up to our house. The back doors opened and our two stragglers trailed out, looking terrified and exhausted. I could see two other boys sitting in the wagon waiting to be dropped off at home. They didn't look too healthy or happy either.

The prodigals were welcomed home with open arms. I don't remember them getting a dressing-down. They were fed, scrubbed, and put to bed, where they dropped into the oblivious, deep sleep of the safe and innocent.

I know that the boys had to appear before Judge Brown for the cottage break-in. Nothing had been disturbed in the place; just a few cans of food were missing. Lew explained to the judge that his little brother had been sick with hunger, and the judge let them all off with a stern warning about respect for the property of others.

The two boys from Theatre Hill were ordered by their parents not to dare associate with the ruffians from Allan Square for the rest of their natural lives.

Having the boys return safely was one of the happiest days of my young life. I hated the Chinese burns and the knuckle hits to the upper arm, but I loved my brothers.

Chapter 4

Jerry and Lew left school at thirteen and eleven to help support the family. Poor little guys, they were only babies themselves, for God's sake. People advised Mom to put us in an orphanage, but she wouldn't even contemplate the thought. Bless her for that; she had guts.

The oldest boy, my "big" brother, Jerry, found a job in a store on Water Street, and Lew used a bike to deliver telegrams. My two youngest brothers were too small to work and I was a girl, so the workforce was sparse on Allan Square.

Every day I left my mother's bed a sodden mess. After the fierce tongue lashing the next morning, during which no feelings were spared, I hung my head in shame and wended my way up Queen's Road toward Presentation Convent, anticipating the wrath of one steely-eyed nun or the other. I was rarely disappointed.

Things were no calmer at school, the big difference being that the sisters all had what seemed to be huge, thick leather straps, and they had no fear of using them. Their mood swings don't surprise me now. Imagine, fifteen or so nuns, all of them experiencing symptoms of PMS or menopause at the same time, and my mother at home, half-starved and worried to death, dealing with five fatherless children, and also with the same symptoms as the nuns. Add the constant fear of sin that was drilled into us, and it's easy to see how a kid's head could get screwed up.

Mine was more screwed up than most of my classmates'.

* * * * *

My screwed-up head manifested itself in some peculiar ways. For one thing, I had a secret fascination with death and its trappings. For some peculiar reason I loved funerals and wakes. One reason for the attraction was that, when the wakes were held at the deceased's home, there was food, and plenty of it. I took my nourishment whenever and however I found it.

There was no problem knowing when someone had died; the window blinds were always drawn. So it was a simple matter of washing my face, combing my hair and knocking at the door of a house with drawn blinds. The house didn't have to be on Allan Square; a nearby neighbourhood one was just as good. The genuine mourners knew that anyone who came to the house was there for the dearly departed. I would stick my hand out and, carefully avoiding the eyes, mumble sincerely, "Sorry for your trouble."

That was the appetizer. The next step was being ushered into the presence of the deceased, whom I had never laid eyes on before this first sad encounter.

I had it down to a science. The human drama kept me to my purpose, that and hunger. Down I'd go on the red velvet kneeler, clasping my hands and staring soulfully into the face of the corpse. Then came the sign of the Cross. At the same time I took note of every stray nostril hair and intently examined the folded hands clasped around the rosary beads. The hands of the deceased always held rosary beads.

Then, after a suitable respectful show of grief, I would gaze reverently at the larger-than-life picture of Jesus with His Sacred Heart, looking down sorrowfully on the casket from His position halfway up the wall. The sacred blood dripping from the heart almost, but not quite, turned me off thoughts of food. Such was my hunger that I barely felt His eyes following my back, as I made my way to an empty chair.

There was always an element of danger involved in these visits. If the visitation was not on our street, how about if they found out that I didn't know a living (or dead) person in the house? You couldn't count the corpse; I felt almost a sense of family for the people in the caskets. At least they'd never be hungry again. If I were found to be impersonating a mourner, would someone grab me by the hair and yank me home to my mother? In spite of my mother's renowned temper, it was a risk I was prepared to take.

Safely settled in a corner chair – I always chose the corner one because I liked to have a wall at my back, less chance of a surprise attack – I raised my eyes and took careful stock of the room. I had already spotted the kitchen on the way in, so there was a little time to kill. After all, I did have some manners, and it would not have been polite to make a lunge in that direction too quickly.

So I'd indulge in a little people watching, always one of my favourite pastimes. It was very entertaining, and nobody paid any attention to the hungry-looking little girl, her dark brown hair combed so neatly, who sat quietly in the corner chair. I watched and waited until my stomach growls became so loud I could hear them and the man sitting next to me gazed at me with a puzzled stare and, wondering, rubbed his own stomach and cast an embarrassed glance around the room.

Through trial and error I'd discovered that the best time to approach the food was when new mourners arrived. Then everyone's attention was taken up with the corpse and the reactions of the new arrivals.

So I'd quietly get up from my chair and follow the smell of food down the hall to the kitchen. Open Sesame! A feast waited – mounds and mounds of sandwiches, china cups and saucers. Sometimes there was even hot soup, usually pea soup because that was the cheapest. Then there was the dessert table, like dying and going to heaven. I was soon stuffed and nearing the peaceful state of oblivion the corpse was enjoying.

One more step remained: getting out the front door without appearing too obvious. Then a large exhale of embalming fluid and an equally large intake of fresh salt air, and I was as good as new – better, in fact.

I could almost imagine the comments when my absence was noted. “Did you see that poor little girl? I wonder who she was?”

“Homely little thing, wasn’t she? She looks like she could use a good meal, God love her!”

God love them, and the corpses, too. God rest all their souls, whoever they were.

I’d already had my good meal, thanks to their earthly leave-taking.

Chapter 5

My childhood on Allan Square was fraught with many fears, one of which was the serious threat of an early demise, but the largest threat was one that became an integral part of my early childhood, the so-called formative years, and actually presented a threat to my very sanity – the infamous coal pound! It had a lock on the door that opened from the outside, of course. The better to lock you in, my dear.

The coal pound was located in the lobby, right off the kitchen. It contained, naturally, the coal for stoking the big Ideal range. The lobby had no light and contained only the cold-water sink.

Did I mention that we had lots of mice in the house, or were they possibly rats? From this distance in time, there's no way I can ever really be sure, but I do know they were bigger than any mice had the right to be, and they reigned supreme, in utter and complete freedom, in the coal pound. There was no light in there, either, as a matter of fact, which might have been a good thing, considering my delicate frame of mind.

The coal pound punishment must have been in place before my father passed away, because I remember him trying to toss my brother Jack into the hellhole. Jack was rigid as a board and screaming his head off. There was no way he was going in there. My father finally turned to my mother and said, "Here, take your brat!" So Jack, God love him, was reprieved, to live in relative safety, until the next time around.

When my turn came for incarceration, there was no possibility of relief; I was pushed in, and I stayed in! My screaming did no good, nor did my pleas for mercy, or at the very least, for a box of matches or a flashlight. I figured I could face down the rats or the mice, but it was the total darkness that really screwed up my head. Nowadays it would be called out-and-out child abuse.

The memory of my first of many sojourns in the coal pound stems from a day I spent downtown with my mother. I was about four years old. I had a ferocious temper as a child and was certainly spoiled, especially by Dad. I began to kick up a racket when Mom did not buy me a certain toy I wanted.

She responded with a few cracks on my ass. I continued the uproar until we rounded the corner of Theatre Hill onto Allan Square and I saw our house. My mother, after struggling up the steep incline of Theatre Hill, dragging and half carrying a violently resisting child, finally stopped to catch her breath. She was dealing with a heart condition, of which I had no knowledge at the time. At that stage of the adventure I'm sure she would have cheerfully tossed me into the enfolding waters of St. John's Harbour.

I had a temper, but I was not stupid. I knew it was time for the piper to be paid. Sure enough, I never made it to the kitchen. Instead, Mom pulled open the door to the coal pound. She thrust me into that dank wintry hole, slammed the door and locked it.

The darkness was all-enveloping, to the point of suffocation. I can't get a handle on how long I was forced to remain in there before merciful release. I do know that I screamed the entire time, curdling cries and sobs only a petrified child can conjure. The constant movement of something in the place stopped my screams periodically. Maybe it was the mice, maybe not. I've always been a good sleeper, but I found no rest in that goddamned coal pound.

When the ritualized coal pound incarcerations began to fall way, I was regularly tossed and locked into Mom's bedroom at suppertime. Her bedroom was directly off the kitchen. Where we cooked is where we ate. The poor man's feast. Slumped on the floor, beating my hands against the locked bedroom door, I screamed my head off as Mom and the boys, unresponsive, silently ate. I guess I eventually became civilized and learned to keep my mouth shut. Maybe.

The face of whoever finally unlocked the door is gone from my memory, never to be recalled, thank God, but I do know there were no comforting hugs, nor any welcoming arms. That would have defeated the purpose of the punishment, I suppose. But God bless me, I sure turned out a fine, poor little bitch, all things considered. The incarcerations ended when we changed from a coal stove to an oil stove. There was no need for a coal pound when we didn't use coal. I used to think maybe somebody noticed that I was in serious danger of losing my mind, but I realized later that was not the fact.

Granted, I came out of it with no bites, unless you count the flea bites, of course. Sure we had fleas, didn't everybody? We had cats, and every cat in the neighbourhood was riddled with fleas.

We took in the stray cats only because of the mice infestations, not from any love of animals, and it was because of the cats that we got the fleas, who liked to sleep in our beds and drink our blood. Bloody vampires, they were. There were no flea collars in those days, I guess. If there were any in our place, they were certainly ineffective. The fleas were jumping, and so were we.

Eventually, the cats got pregnant. I watched with wonder as their stomachs distended, and I was totally amazed that eating fleas and mice could make an animal so fat.

Naturally, I discovered the real reason for their big bellies soon enough. Both cats went into labour in the night, very quietly; not even a moan do I remember hearing.

Then these cute little balls of life suddenly appeared with their eyes firmly closed. It was lucky for them their eyes were closed, because as quickly as they were born, they were plunged into a pail of cold water and heartlessly dispatched to cat heaven. Right away! Hardly a chance to take a first breath, and certainly no time to grow much fur!

My God, how did I ever manage to take to motherhood when my kids were born! The horror of it all ran a close second to the coal pound as far as trauma goes, and a narrow third to another experience of seeing a chicken/hen run circles around our backyard with its head cut off and blood squirting every which way.

The memories, God help me, are in Technicolour.

Chapter 6

When my brothers and I were kids, before Dad's death, we all called our parents by their Christian names. Dad was Lew and Mom was Dot. That's just the way it was, kind of strange, really. None of my friends called their parents by their first names, but it just seemed natural to us.

We were raised in what could, in a loose sense, be called a bilingual family. Everyone in the house, to some degree, spoke two languages, "garden variety" English and Pig Latin. I know that I spoke and understood it better than my parents realized. I always knew that it was not a game. My nickname, "Granny," had not been given without good cause. I heard, saw and understood everything.

I saw in Dad's eyes, as he sat on the side of the bed, his fathomless grief at our imminent separation. We both realized we would never again, in the flesh, feel his pulse beating with mine, as my hand clung tightly to his thumb. To this day thinking about Pig Latin still acts as a conduit to the consuming grief of that little girl.

As in most families, we had nicknames. My brother Lew was called "Junie," to separate him from Dad I guess. God help him; talk about Johnny Cash's "A Boy Named Sue." Poor Lew spent most of his childhood beating the daylights out of anybody who called him Junie.

Unfortunately that included me, but he was a bit gentler with me than he was with the others. Mostly I wound up being cornered in some part of the kitchen, on the receiving end of an expertly executed Chinese burn. Anybody who has brothers knows that a Chinese burn means twisting the flesh on the wrists in different directions. More than once, too. If you wanted to make Lew angry, you called him "Junie" and then you ran like hell.

Lew was my second-oldest brother and he had a voice like a nightingale from his earliest years. I can still remember my Dad giving him some coins to sing "Bendemeer's Stream" for visitors. He was also a great forager, always bringing home something or other that he had found in his travels. He often wandered up to Signal Hill and was late getting back for supper. When Mom demanded to know his whereabouts he invariably replied:

"Up to the Labrador, looking for gold!"

He is a prospector now, and a pretty successful one. He is credited with starting the uranium rush in Labrador.

One time, Lew brought home packages of chocolate candies. He'd found them down in McMurdo's Lane, by the side door of McMurdo's Drugstore. We were all over the moon with excitement. We totally gorged ourselves on the slightly bitter stuff. We soon discovered that what we were eating was Ex-Lax. They looked like candy, but the laxative effect was all Ex-Lax.

That ended his exploits for a few days. As a matter of fact, we all had the runs, and most movement in the flat, was slowed down to a crawl to the washroom. After that episode, anything Lew brought home was examined carefully, if it looked in any way edible.

He did, however, do his bit in keeping the home fires burning, by traversing the neighbourhood and checking the houses where coal had been delivered. Anything that was sitting on the ground outside those houses was carefully collected by my brother and dumped into our coal pound – fortunately this coal delivery by Lew was never made at any of the times when I was in residence in the bloody hole. It would only have been small showers of coal at a time, anyway, so I wouldn't have been injured even if I had been there. I would simply have choked to death. Such were the mercies for which I soon learned to thank my Maker.

When I look back at the efforts my brother made to give us a little extra warmth, it makes me smile.

My brother Jack, God love him, often got me in big trouble. Mom couldn't stand to hear me screaming out "Dot!" and she heard it a lot. My side of the story was never told. One day Mom was feeling unwell and taking a rest in her bedroom, which was right off the kitchen. Jack was over by the window, coming slowly toward me, brandishing a very large and sharp kitchen knife. I remember his face was screwed into a horrible mask of destruction – mine. I would have preferred death by natural causes. I don't think that he really intended to kill me, though, just to put the fear of God into my soul. He needn't have bothered; there was already enough fear in my heart to keep me on my knees for a week, at least.

Anyway, before I knew what was happening, Mom had made a remarkably swift recovery and found her way out of the bedroom, heading in my direction. I'm sure she felt that she had to shut up my screaming, or else go mad.

By that time, Jack had put the knife safely out of sight and had his normal, loving brother face plastered on. To make this part of a long story short, I got the rounds of the kitchen (a good beating) and a damn good tongue-lashing to boot. Jack came out of it looking like a saint. He always was her pet; he never seemed to get into any trouble. He was also a Chinese burn expert, with me on the receiving end. I worshipped him. I suppose that would be called "battered-sister syndrome" in mental health terms, and was probably a portent of things to come – like panic disorder maybe?

In the meantime, all the neighbourhood bullies were scared of my brothers and ran like hell when I threatened to call them. They protected me fiercely from outsiders. No one was allowed to lay a finger on me. I took full advantage of the Murphy strength at my back.

* * * * *

My stepfather, Bill, was one hell of a tough cookie when drunk. His personality wasn't so hot when stone sober, either. He must have been on his best behaviour when he was courting my mother, because he sure fooled her. I guess he had his ways, even with me.

I remember the odd shekel being pressed into my hand once in a while as he held me on his knee. When they married and he took up permanent residence, there were no more signs of pseudo-affection from him. I received no more shekels. I was tossed off his knee in no time at all, and I remained off.

The fact that I had flatly refused Mom's invitation to call him "Dad" might have had something to do with his lack of enchantment with the only daughter of the house.

His alcoholic rages were awesome in the terror they inspired. The first time I saw him foam at the mouth, I promised myself that he would never take the place of my father.

As far as I knew, only dogs foamed at the mouth, vicious dogs. I was afraid of dogs when I was a kid, and I was afraid of Bill.

One Saturday night my friend Moll and I were sitting on my front steps, telling ghost stories, when Moll nudged me and pointed to the corner of Allan Square and Theatre Hill.

Sure enough, there he was, listing heavily from side to side, staggering his way toward the mayhem he must have begun to plan as soon as he spotted our house.

I was quite surprised to see him coming home using "shank's mare." He sometimes spared his feet and arrived by taxi.

We scattered, as he tripped his way up the steps and slammed the door viciously. Moll headed for her home across the street and I snuck through the door, turning and entering the front room instead of braving the kitchen. I went from the front room through my bedroom and into Mom's room. I could see the kitchen and hear the action from there.

It had rained heavily that day, and the kitchen floor was covered with wet newspapers, towels, and anything else that could be used to soak up the water. The backyard sloped downward toward the house, the soil was thin, and there was nothing to stop the flow. Every time it rained we watched helplessly as the water cleared the doorstep and began to lap around our heels.

This particular night the wet floor seemed to really infuriate my stepfather. His feet kept getting tangled in the soaking newspapers, and his already unsteady mobility was quickly becoming even more impaired.

There were dozens of grey wool work socks strung around the kitchen on makeshift clotheslines. As part of my childhood duties, I had washed and hung them earlier in the day. Every time Bill moved a few steps, the wet paper under his feet curled into balls and a couple of the damp socks brushed his face. I remember thinking to myself that the whole situation was definitely not looking good for us.

Mom had just placed his dinner on the cherry red and white oilcloth that covered the kitchen table, when the front door opened, and I recognized my brother Jack's footsteps coming down the hallway. Jack was about thirteen then.

"Go back!" I screamed soundlessly at my brother. "Go back, for the love and honour of Christ!"

My stepfather chose the arrival of Jack to toss his dinner plate right up over his head. He accompanied this exercise with a vicious scream of rage.

Some of the fried bologna, mustard, onions and mashed potatoes stuck to the ceiling, but a good portion of it rained down on the grey work socks. After spending the entire afternoon washing those sluttin' socks I was none too pleased at the turn things were taking, but I could only watch helplessly. "Sluttin'" by the way, will not be found in a dictionary. It's a family colloquialism, courtesy of my Uncle Leo. It means exactly the same thing as it's infamous cousin "fuckin'."

Bill stood there like a demented avenging angel, pointing his messy fingers at Jack. I knew what his next words would be. I had heard them before.

He stared at Mom, his eyes red with rage, foam just beginning to ooze from his gaping mouth, and screamed loud enough to be heard in the street.

"That one is a goddamn bastard!"

Of course those were fighting words, and Jack's Irish was immediately up. He made a flying leap toward his tormentor, and I heard the harsh sound of flesh hitting flesh. Poor Jack wound up with a sizzler of a shiner and was tossed unceremoniously into the bedroom.

I put my hands to my lips and shook my head. I did not want to be discovered, and I definitely lacked the courage of my brother.

With that, Mom went into action and ranted at Bill, calling him every name in the book. Some of them she had learned from him.

I was amazed at her guts or her stupidity. In her place I would have run like hell. Her attack only made him angrier.

"There's only one bastard here, you son of a bitch! And it's not my son!" she screamed at him.

With that, he totally lost whatever little bit of common sense he might have owned before he hit Allan Square that night. Everything on the table, Carnation milk, butter, salt and pepper, cups and saucers, and the boiling hot teapot was swiped off with one vicious swing of his powerful arm, hitting the floor with a godawful racket to join the soaking papers on the kitchen floor.

Next to go was the ramshackle cabinet that held our paltry store of extra dishes. It crashed onto the floor with the sound of breaking dishes and shattering wood. The noise was deafening.

My mother was cornered over by the kitchen window. I watched as he flexed his arms, all the while screaming obscenities, in preparation for getting a grip on the heavy wooden table. He lifted it off the floor and turned it arse-over-kettle.

By this time Jack was screaming bloody blue murder and trying to get into the kitchen to help our mother. The door was blocked. She was fighting Bill tooth and nail, reaming off some of the finest oaths I had ever heard in my eleven years. I would have sworn before that night I had heard them all before. But you live and learn.

"You only married me to get a fuckin' meal ticket for yer youngsters, you slut!" he screamed through the foam trickling down his chin.

"Goddamn right!" she yelled back at him. "Why else would anyone marry the likes of you anyway? Why don't you go back to your fat sister where you belongs, you rotten whoremaster. You old tamer!"

Whoremaster? Tamer? I resolved to look up those words. I had not heard them before. I sat back in my helplessness and pondered their meanings.

The one good thing to come out of the mess on the litter-strewn floor was that the smashed furniture prevented him from reaching Mom to add more bruises to the ones already inflicted during their initial confrontation.

Right about then we heard a commotion in the front hall. The neighbours had obviously come to life. Three big, hardy policemen charged into the kitchen, took one look at the mess, and collared Bill. He suddenly turned quiet as a lamb and did not resist as they dragged him down the hall. They pushed him roughly into the waiting Black Maria.

By this time Jack and I had made our way through my bedroom to the front room window, and we screamed at him as the Black Maria pulled away, headed toward the lock-up. We were glad to see the back end of him.

Poor Jack, his eye red and swollen, ran back to the kitchen looking for Mom. I followed him. We found her sitting in the corner by the kitchen stove. Tears were trickling down her face.

She was exhausted. She had fought the good fight, and we all knew that it would not be the last one she'd have to fight. She had let our stepfather know, to Jack's gratification, that, by God, there were no bastards in our family.

Bill spent two nights in jail and appeared before the magistrate on Monday morning. My mother refused to appear, so they had to let him out. She said she would not lower herself.

So he came back to drink and fight again.

Chapter 7

My mother was not a well woman. I have a faded picture of her with her first-born, my brother Jerry, in her arms. He was a plump baby of about three months and she is smiling down on him adoringly. He became the handsome boy she was to refer to, after my father's death, and until her own death, as her "Rock."

In the old black-and-white shot, faded now to sepia, my Mom is dressed in a silk print dress and her long, black hair is flowing loose, natural highlights glinting in the sun. The small picture is framed and sitting on my bureau. She looks young, vibrant and very happy.

She always told me that a woman's first child is her only child of love. I didn't ask which emotions the rest of us had been conceived in. There would have been no point, after all. As she was so fond of saying, "When hunger comes in the door, love flies out the window."

It was in the days before social assistance and birth control, and I have no doubt that she was right.

In another picture, after my birth, she is a stark contrast of before and after. Aged beyond her years, sick and tired, she is sitting on a blanket in the backyard, with my brother Jack by her side. He is about three years old. My mother is looking into the camera with an expression on her face of total exhaustion and worry, but still a half-smile plays around her lips.

One of the reasons for her ravaged health was certainly my birth. I remember hearing her tell the story, before I was noticed and shooed from the room. I always got escorted to the door at the good parts.

"She almost killed me!" and then bang, the door closed behind me. I was left to wonder what in God's name I had done to nearly kill my mother.

"I would sooner have a dozen boys than one girl!" With that statement I was again sent, wondering and worried, into the fresh air of Allan Square. It took me years to get a handle on the fact that it was my actual physical arrival in this vale of sorrows that had almost done her in.

My mother had arrived in St. John's from her home in Tickle Cove, Bonavista Bay. Her eldest sister, Mary, had a job as a housemaid in a grand house on Rennie's Mill Road, and my mother joined her there. She was sixteen years old, and I don't think the work was easy. It was among these affluent people that she developed a taste for "cow's milk" as opposed to Carnation canned milk. She always used fresh milk for her tea. She also became fond of "real" butter, as opposed to margarine, and used it on her toast for the rest of her life. She had to hide it from me; I had a taste for it, too.

One August, on the way to the Regatta, the annual boat races held in St. John's, my father and I were walking to Quidi Vidi Lake. He pointed out a large, majestic tree in front of one of the big houses. "That's where I used to wait for your mother," he said with a smile.

Rennie's Mill Road was a far cry from Allan Square, and it must have taken a bit of adjustment on her part. But when you're with the man you love, anything is possible and she was, for a while, able to enjoy her fresh butter and cow's milk.

Along with her ferocious temper and kick-ass attitude, my mother also had a well-developed sense of humour. She loved a smutty joke and caught the funny side of many harrowing situations that would have made a lesser woman cry. When I got older and began telling my own richly coloured stories of the street, she often said my sense of humour was the result of genes from her side of the family.

If my mother ever turned back to revisit my father's

dying, she didn't bring any of us along for the ride. As a matter of fact, she didn't talk about him at all and I felt a desperate need to do just that, talk.

The only way I knew she missed him even worse than I did was when, before her second marriage, I went home from school for lunch to find her crying at the kitchen table. She must have been insane with worry about providing even enough food for us to survive. I'll never know because she didn't talk about it. "Let the dead rest!" was her command. I didn't want to let him rest. I wanted my father back.

The exact period when the man who was to become my stepfather made his appearance on the scene is locked out of my memory. It seems that he was just there one day, and he didn't appear to be in any hurry to leave. He must have been very gutsy or a little crazy, to take on the widow of his friend, along with her four sons and a daughter. Perhaps he made a pact with his old friend to take care of the family when the end came.

* * * * *

One of the first tasks my stepfather undertook, when he became embedded in the war zone that was our home, was to rid the place of mice. He laid traps and put down poisons with zeal and relish. Those mice were going! And go they did.

Every morning there were fresh corpses in the killing fields. The cats got fat and lazy. Little did they know they were next on his list. After all, how to get rid of the fleas without first getting rid of their carriers?

He cold-bloodedly dumped each of the cats into a cloth brin bag and took off at a brisk pace down Allan Square and over Theatre Hill toward the harbour. I watched gloomily from the doorstep, wondering if perhaps I might wind up sharing the fate of the cats. I didn't particularly care for them, but I was sure that death by drowning was a cruel and unjust punishment for them and that it wouldn't be too cheerful for me, either. I must admit, though, I was looking forward to not having to share my bed with the fleas. It was getting more difficult to hide the bite marks. I did have some pride, after all.

However, a cloth bag and the harbour were not to be my fate. Instead, when school broke for the summer I was sent to St. Mary's Bay, to spend two months with my aunt Mary and her brood. I knew and liked them all, so I looked forward to it.

I might have been spoiling the honeymoon period for my mother and her new husband. Another big problem was where they were going to put me to sleep. I couldn't really continue to sleep in my mother's bed and pee all over her as I had done in the past; I also could not sleep in their room. So clearly something had to be done. I prayed nightly that the peeing would soon stop. I was nearly ten, so I lived in hope, praying that I wouldn't die in despair or be killed by my soggy mother early one chilly morning. I wouldn't have blamed her anyway if she had been tempted to do away with me. Waking up wet when you haven't done the peeing is a hell of a way to start the day.

I went to St. Mary's in a taxi. The roads were not paved, instead they were liberally sprinkled with potholes the size of moon craters. There was no money in pre-Confederation days for much road paving. There were also passengers smoking in the car, and I was nearly suffocated, coughing like a fiend the whole trip. The taxi was crowded and the ride was bumpy, very hard on my (at that time) skinny bum, but we did arrive in one piece.

I had a wonderful time with my cousins, making the hay, rolling around the barn, picking the vegetables for supper, and hunting for bakeapples on the marshes. The water down the hill from my aunt's house moved clean and clear. It was an incredible blue, heaven to the eyes of the townie cousin who was used to the septic green of St. John's Harbour.

I remember my mother sent a care package containing oranges, apples, and assorted other goodies. I almost died of shock and surprise. It was a good feeling.

By the time I got back to St. John's I was brown as a berry, full of freckles and scratching like crazy. You do that when you're lousy, and they didn't come any lousier than I was after the only summer vacation of my childhood. I don't know who infected whom, and it sure doesn't matter now. As a point of interest, I didn't notice anyone scratching when I arrived. They were sure scratching by the time I left, though.

The first thing my mother did, after using home remedies for delousing, was to hand me a dollar and order me up around the corner to Whelan's barbershop. I was given strict instructions to ask for a shingle cut. I didn't know exactly what a "shingle" cut meant. But I soon learned as I watched the lengths of my long dark hair float to the floor. Then I felt the cold steel of the clippers on my neck, and I nearly died of despair. I looked like that bane of my childhood – a boy! It was not a good welcome-home omen.

The flat on Allan Square was, by the time I returned home, totally cleansed of vermin. The mice, fleas, cats and lice were all gone and the place reeked from liberal scrubbings with Jeyes Fluid and water. Jeyes Fluid was a disinfectant in popular use at the time. It is now out of favour, and probably rightly so. God only knows what was in it. There were also other changes to the flat.

The kitchen had been freshly painted, there was new, brightly patterned oilcloth on the table and new canvas covered the floor. My brothers and I had somehow managed to survive the vermin purge. We were still there, with a good possibility of staying. I had new sleeping quarters, the little room off my mother's bedroom. It had no door, only a curtain. I mention that because it got on my nerves at the time – this from someone who had spent her nights sleeping with other people's feet in her face. In my new room I slept on a folding cot. Strangely enough, I did not pee the bed there.

There was a window, a chair, and an old trunk in my new cubicle. I was not supposed to go near the trunk, but of course I did at the first opportunity. I found a pile of Mass cards tied with a blue ribbon. They were from my father's wake and made me unbearably sad. There was also a blue knitted baby bonnet, sweater, and booties. They'd belonged to the baby brother who had died before his third month.

I remember my father bringing his little body into the kitchen, and that was where he was waked, in a small white casket. I picked up his little leg and let it drop back into the casket. He looked like a tiny sleeping doll, and I wanted to see if he would move when prodded. He did not.

The old trunk also held photo albums filled with shots of my father in his youth and his family. I did not recognize any of my relatives because I had never seen them before. I don't think the Bronx was a very upscale neighbourhood, but it really didn't matter to me at the time. They were, to my mind, exotic, mysterious strangers who reeked of mystery and money because they lived in the States.

My father had gone with them initially but simply could not shake Newfoundland from his soul. He had met our mother before he left for parts unknown, and if not for that fact, he might have stayed in the States and died there, as did all of his close relatives.

His sister, my aunt Hann, wrote faithfully, always addressing her letters to me. In a way she kept my father's memory alive for me. I was a grown woman when she passed away, and the letters and small gifts kept arriving faithfully throughout her life. I loved her dearly, even before I got the chance to meet her when I was eighteen and took a trip to New York. She was a link to my father.

There is still a chamber in my heart for her, in gratitude for the beautiful, unconditional love she sent me. Of course she only knew me from letters and, I had never peed on her.

Chapter 8

In my mother's bedroom a picture of the Sacred Heart gazed down from one wall. A bronze, crucified Christ hung over the bed, and a statue of the Virgin, complete with lighted votive candle, was enshrined on a dresser. On a shelf next to the bed stood my stepfather's statue of St. Thérèse, the "Little Flower."

My stepfather was a short, blocky man with wide shoulders, muscular arms, large, rheumy blue eyes and a massive balding head. People said he led with that head during his many street brawls. When he married Mom, he took his brawling off the sidewalks and brought it into our house. Saturday nights, after he grew used to his new family status, became a free-for-all, complete with the arrival of the police. The swearing and foaming at the mouth, which were part of his alcohol-induced rages, were accompanied by the crash of dishes, the overturning of furniture and Mom's goading cry:

"Get the hell out of here. Go back to where you came from, you rotten bastard!"

After he was gone and the place was looking somewhat normal, a strange quiet descended on the kitchen, as the survivors sat in the dark, each lost in thought, basking in the warmth and light from the big Ideal coal range. Through Mom's bedroom door, the shadows cast by the flickering light of the Virgin's votive candle added to the cozy atmosphere.

He usually arrived back in the house after his stay in the lock-up with peace offerings: nylons and fruits for Mom and chocolates for anyone who had the stamina to fight for one. Then he'd sit at the kitchen table and guzzle a concoction of raw eggs and milk, which was supposed to "fix him up," presumably replacing whatever nutrients his system had lost as a result of the booze. I guess the mixture worked, because he always demonstrated new energy after swigging it down. He went through the place like a dose of salts. Floors were scrubbed and liberally disinfected with Jeyes Fluid. I was thrilled when I saw my stepfather on his knees; it meant I didn't have to scrub the floors that week.

My mother always said, "We don't learn from him, he learns from us. He never had a good mother to raise him. Anyway, he promised he's going to take the pledge. Tomorrow he's going up to see Father McGrath to swear off the stuff."

But he continued boozing, changing his mind about the pledge, saying he had no desire to be like all the other hypocrites, eating the church on Sundays and stealing the eyes out of people's heads the rest of the week.

Drunk or sober, my stepfather joined my mother in inventiveness and managed to come up with a new name for me.

I still don't know what kind of an impression I was giving to my family – it must have been something about my attitude. Besides Lady Alderdice, Lady Bowring, and Madam, I now had to acknowledge and respond to "aide-de-camp."

My stepfather began to refer to me as my mother's aide-de-camp. Whenever he wanted to visit his sister, he'd ask Mom to go with him, but she always declined. There was no way she was going to dirty her feet with the tough soil of his former neighbourhood.

"Can I take your aide-de-camp, then?" She wouldn't dare refuse.

Before I knew it I'd find myself on the streetcar headed for his sister's place. I didn't mind. She worked as a supervisor at a biscuit factory, and she had an unlimited supply of loose, sweet biscuits in her cupboards.

My mother was moody as hell. I mulled hopelessly over the mystery of her disposition. I could never make any sense out of it. When I was older I realized that there was a name for it: PMS.

In spite of the presence of St. Thérèse, the drinking continued. Without fail, the same scenario unfolded week after week, his "spavilized" homecoming, the knock down, drag-out fight, Mom's gutsy voice matching his, pitch for rising pitch, the arrival of the policemen clinging to the back of the Black Maria, their short uniform capes blowing in the wind.

My stepfather's departure for jail was the last act of the tragedy and to me it was the finest one, like some form of Divine retribution.

Each time the cops came for him I concluded that maybe St. Thérèse really did answer prayers. He was gone, wasn't he? Mom was peaceful, kind of all fought out, and we were safely out of the attack loop for another night.

We remained the talk of the street. I never did tell Mom or my brothers that I was the one who called the police every week.

That's why I knew about the policemen's capes flying in the wind. My friend Moll and I watched and waited for them. She was the one person who knew my secret, and she was pledged to silence. Her house had the only phone on the street. After the call was made, she and I peeked through the lace curtains and waited. What a beautiful sight those policemen were! I've loved men in uniform ever since.

One night the routine inexplicably changed. Drunk as usual, my stepfather staggered in the front door and made a wavering beeline for their bedroom. We thought he was sick, maybe going to lie down; if so, this would have made a nice change, but he didn't have anything so mild on his mind. Mom, my brother Jack and I watched in horror as he made a grab for St. Thérèse and dragged her from her shelf. God only knows what was going through his mind.

"Jesus, Mary and Joseph! What, in the name of Christ,

are you doing? Give me back the Little Flower, right now, you drunken blaguard!"

The Virgin's votive candle flickered dangerously as my stepfather staggered out the bedroom door. He bumped into tables, chairs and walls on his way down the hallway, finally safely manoeuvring his way down the front steps.

Jack and I ran to the door, screeching after him, begging him to give up St. Thérèse. No luck. He turned, shook his fist at us and shouted, "Get back in the house, ye little buggers, or I'll have yer guts for garters!"

That was enough for us. We ran into the house to check on Mom, who was sitting on the bed, staring at St. Thérèse's empty shelf. When she saw us, she sprang up and into action, grabbing each of us by the arm and pushing us toward the front door.

"Now! For the love and honour of God! Get to hell's fiery flames out that door, the two of ye, and bring her back. Do ye hear me? Don't let him get away! He'll bring bad luck on the house, taking St. Thérèse. What in God's name do he intend to do with her? Now! I'm chargin' ye! Get! Bring back the Little Flower or don't darken the door this night of our Lord!"

We took off into the night, flying down Allan Square and around the corner to Theatre Hill. We could see the man of the house, his navigational skills impaired by an excessive intake of bootlegger's rum, halfway down the hill. We began to trail him, careful not to get too close. Every now and then the statue slid farther down my stepfather's chest. Theatre Hill turned into New Gower Street, an area that was forbidden to us at nighttime.

"Look!" Jack grabbed my arm. "He's stopping in front of the Ritz tavern. Maybe he's going to take her in there? He wouldn't dare. Would he?"

Instead of going into the tavern, my stepfather planked himself down on the steps leading to it and propped the Little Flower between his legs. He began fumbling in his pockets and pulled out a pack of Lucky Strikes. After several attempts to light one, he finally succeeded. We ducked into a doorway about three houses away from the Ritz and took quick peeks, trying to anticipate his next move.

Our stepfather was on his feet again, taking two steps forward and three steps back, weaving toward the corner of Adelaide and New Gower streets.

When he reached the intersection at Adelaide, his legs buckled and his head fell forward. It looked as if he intended to take a nap right there on the sidewalk, or maybe even die. He still had a death grip on the statue.

My brother whipped the Little Flower from his arms. We didn't look back until we were at the beginning of Queen's Road. By then we were both gasping for air, and I had to take a turn carrying the Little Flower because Jack had a stitch in his side.

From where we were resting we could see all the way down New Gower to Adelaide Street. "Shit!" Jack said. "Look at that!"

There *she* was, at the corner of Adelaide Street, in all her shiny glory – the Black Maria. The double doors were open and two tall policemen – they were always tall in those days – were bent over our stepfather, prodding him none too gently. The next thing we knew, they'd dumped him into the back of the paddy wagon. It took off down Duckworth Street toward the cop shop.

Jack nodded. "They does that with the drunkards, when they finds them asleep on New Gower Street."

Chapter 9

Two years before Newfoundland's union with Canada, I was in fifth grade (B class) at Presentation Convent in St. John's. Around our house on Allan Square there were rumours that *it* was definitely going to happen.

The word was that Newfoundland, if she had any sense at all, would give up the hardship of going it alone, and then we'd all get the baby bonus, old-age pensions and all sorts of other goodies.

My mother was particularly interested in the baby bonus. I developed a fine sense of self-worth with the very thought of the union with Canada. My mere presence in our house now meant money: cold, hard cash monthly.

I was almost certain that the baby bonus would encourage my mother to wallop me in the head with a *dry* dishcloth instead of a wet one; less chance of brain damage, coma, or maybe even death, I reasoned to myself.

She desperately wanted to collect, so it seemed that I might survive my home life.

That fact gave me a small measure of peace. Purely in the interests of self-preservation in 1947, I became somewhat partial to all things Canadian, and I began to develop an interest in politics. Reading the newspaper before school each morning, trying to figure out when my money would be coming through, became an integral part of my day.

It was a different matter in school; the ground was much shakier. Mother Bridget, our teacher, was not in favour of union with Canada. Confederation, she warned us in ominous tones, would cause Newfoundland to lose its denominational school system, and we would all go to hell in a handbasket if that happened.

She was just a little ahead of her time. Anyway, we were all warned to advise our parents of the coming loss of a Catholic education and I dutifully did so, but it didn't make a dent in my mother.

This left me in a bit of a dilemma as far as school was concerned. I was desperately anxious to survive that year in grade five. Some days it could get a little iffy. Mother Bridget didn't lower herself to use a wet *or* a dry dishcloth. Secreted in her desk was a thick leather strap, its very appearance enough to strike fear in the heart of any child.

I definitely did not want to make her angry, so I kept any precocious knowledge I had about politics to myself. Survival at home and in school was the name of the game in the good old days – the bottom line.

One particular morning in May of 1947, Mother Bridget, ramrod straight in spite of her seventy-odd years, stood in front of her class of fifth-grade girls. Her complexion, normally pale above the austere black of her long habit, was flushed a delicate pink. When our attention was completely assured, which didn't take too long, we were advised sternly that we were expecting a visitor. At the announcement a small ripple of excitement ran through the girls. We quickly controlled our emotions. *A visitor!*

Visitors, in my convent school days, provided a rare and welcome break from the constant rules and regulations imposed by the nuns. Any break at all was eagerly anticipated, even if it only lasted a few minutes. Mother Bridget, God love her, although she was a dedicated religious, probably needed the break even more than we did.

We were the B class, after all, – short attention span and all that – and we invariably gave her a good run for her money. In the grading system of the Presentation Convent, the letter B definitely did not mean "bright." Personally, I always figured I had wound up in that class as a direct result of too many clouts on the head with that wet dishcloth, the trauma of my father's early death and the madhouse I had lived in during the worst of my stepfather's drinking. Time alone would tell.

Mother Bridget, her mere presence an intimidation, was a veteran of many B classes; strict but fair, she knew exactly how to handle us. She kept a very tight rein on the classroom, and little went on without her knowledge.

Normally, she would have been able to guarantee exactly how each of her girls would perform in any given circumstance; had she been wearing a different dress she might have been inclined to safely put money on it. But even "Bridget," as we disrespectfully referred to her, was capable of being taken by surprise.

That long-ago morning our class very quickly became revved up for the anticipated visitor break. We knew it would be happening fairly soon, because a student from another class had been sent along to warn Mother Bridget. This practice of sending a runner ahead was designed to prevent the possibility of the newcomer seeing the next classroom – God forbid – in anything less than perfect form.

The reputation of the teacher, the convent, the church and the world depended on perfect order in the classroom. Each and every visitor was of prime and equal importance at the convent school. We believed this to be gospel. Desks cleared, hands folded, mercifully free from schoolwork for a short while, we were ready.

At this stage of the game, we didn't have a clue as to the identity of the guest. When told to tidy our desks earlier in the morning, we had been advised, in Mother Bridget's best no-nonsense manner, not to bother asking any questions. We were to be seen and, under pain of God knows what, definitely not heard, unless, by some very remote chance, we were directly addressed.

As we waited, the classroom was ominously quiet, except for the occasional rattle of Bridget's long rosary beads and every now and then a nerve-racking crackle from her snowy, starched wimple. Oversized black rosary beads, intertwined with an intimidating strip of black leather, cascaded from her belt down the length of her long skirt.

This particular morning, the morning of *the visitor*, we were safe. Bridget's hands were demurely tucked into the voluminous sleeves of her habit. We needed fear no expert knuckle chops for the time being. At the front of the classroom, Mother Bridget did not noticeably move a muscle, but her eyes, small, dark and keenly intelligent, constantly roved over each of the four rows of compliant uniformed girls.

All eyes were dutifully riveted on the front of the classroom, where our super-sensitized leader was stationed; she was looking exactly like the pictures we had seen of the much-revered St. Thérèse of Avila. For our part we behaved like little angels, or maybe little robots. We might have been the B class, but there was no shortage of common sense in that classroom, and we were smart enough that morning not to make any sudden moves.

There was also the classroom door to be monitored for the anticipated arrival of our mysterious visitor. The door was a wooden one with a tiny, square window set in about three-quarters of the way up. You could say that window was a bit like the peephole in a prisoner's cell. I didn't notice the prisoner aspect of the window at that time, but I guess things really do fall into place with the perspective of maturity.

I turned my eyes to the little window in the classroom door and waited for the arrival of our visitor. The door opened, and the mystery was finally over. All other visitors were wiped from my mind. I was lost!

He was a *beautiful* young priest. He was dressed in regulation garb, black and white clerical collar, and a long, black cassock buttoned all the way down the front. I decided, right then and there, that our visitor could definitely not be from Newfoundland.

As far as I was concerned we didn't have any priests that young in Newfoundland, and if they were there, I figured somebody had to be keeping them away from the convent. The priest who came to our house once a year to collect the "dues" certainly did not look like this one. I was entranced and almost in love, although I knew it was hopeless and maybe even a sin. Wasn't he married to God, or was that Mother Bridget who had taken the vow as a bride of God? Anyway, he was definitely off limits – but what a sight!

To add to my idea of his strange origins, the young priest had a wonderful tan, and his "Good morning, girls" flowed in a strange and exotic accent, a bit like the accents of some of the Yanks from neighbouring Fort Pepperrell.

This young priest had the added attributes of beautiful brown eyes, a fine set of straight, white teeth and a full head of dark, curly hair. He appeared to be a very calm, friendly person and showed definite promise of providing a highly interesting morning diversion.

My none-too-illustrious position in the class seating arrangement was in the last seat of the fourth row of desks. The B class was seated by merit, smart girls in the front. Nobody dared to think discrimination in those days, and besides, I was a fatalist. Mother Bridget had intimated a good few times exactly what she thought of my academic possibilities As for me? Well, I had no reason to doubt her judgment and I liked my back seat in the B class just fine. The safety of a wall was behind me, and a window provided a soothing perspective of the convent garden's gently swaying lilac trees. What more could a non-performer want? Some might say there was no lower place for me to go, but on that particular day I was glad of my position. It left me free to openly inspect our handsome young priest, and I was far enough away so that Mother Bridget might not be able to pick up on the shine in my eyes.

The darling man, having given his name, stood patiently waiting for a follow-up from Mother Bridget. She was blushing up a fine old storm and doing a fair bit of staring herself at this fine specimen of humanity. However, her years of rigorous training and physical denial stood her in good stead. She soon rallied and offered a nice little background sketch on the handsome young priest.

My first impressions regarding his origins were proven correct. The man was definitely not a Newfoundlander; he was a foreigner! This fact was confirmed from Mother Bridget's own sacred lips. He was a Jesuit priest from *Canada*, the frozen wasteland across the Gulf of St. Lawrence. The place, which, if my mother had any say in the matter, would soon be calling Newfoundlanders *family* and sending us the baby bonus!

Almost as good as any Yank, I thought to myself. Soon a map was pulled down over the blackboard and an impromptu geography lesson followed, introducing us to the vastness of Canada. Newfoundland, independently adrift in the vast Atlantic, suddenly seemed to be just a hop, skip and a jump away from the priest's homeland. There was an excited flutter of May hair ribbons and a warning frown from Mother Bridget. She shot the class a stern look and, rosary rattling and wimple crackling, took her seat on the raised platform in front of the blackboard.

My attention was fully riveted on the front of the classroom, on the flashing white teeth and the sparkling eyes of our wonderful visitor. I was not alone; every restless May ribbon settled quietly as the priest's willing captive audience waited respectfully. The atmosphere in the classroom grew heavy with anticipation. It was obvious the young man knew how to work a crowd. Mother Bridget squirmed delicately in her seat, causing the rosary beads to rattle discreetly and the starched wimple to emit only a slight crackle.

In true missionary fashion, the Jesuit's eyes roved over the four identical rows of navy blue uniforms, each one adorned with white collars and cuffs, and finally rested for a few special seconds on a number of randomly selected blue May ribbons.

Obviously satisfied with our rapt attention, he pushed his hands into the pockets of his black cassock, spread his legs apart and rocked back and forth on his heels. Mother Bridget never did that! I was captivated.

The cleric from Canada definitely held the floor, and without more ado he launched into a compelling story about a teenaged-girl martyr in the northern reaches of the far-away, savage country of Canada. The victim's name escapes me now, but her story was a great choice for a convent school. As far as I was concerned, his accent added to the drama of the tale.

He went into graphic detail about her martyrdom at the hands of the savage heathens and concluded that this maiden was pleasing in the eyes of God and well on her way to sainthood. The inference was that we too could be martyrs. Not one of us dared to yell out "Pass!" or to scream for mercy. As the spellbinding story and its short follow-up sermon drew to a close, a collective sense of Catholic guilt, nurtured carefully by the nuns since kindergarten days, washed afresh over every bowed head.

The depression was very real. My attention was drawn back to the cleric from Canada; after spinning the tale of suffering and tragic early death to its agonizing and predictable end, he was again casually rocking on his heels. "Any questions?" His tone was cheerful and his white teeth glistened as his eyes fanned the room in anticipation.

The class had suffered enough already. To Mother Bridget's disgust nobody took the bait; a shamed rosary rattle and an angry wimple crackle came from her direction.

The young priest, however, was an optimist. Continuing his rhythmic heel rocking and flashing a wide warm smile, he went on to his next question.

"Now girls! Can anyone tell me the name of the Prime Minister of Canada?"

Mother Bridget wiped her eyes shakily and gazed tiredly toward her only hope, the smart B girls ranged in each first seat of the four rows of desks. The priest's hands were joined in what could have been interpreted as a praying pose. He had lovely hands.

While waiting for one of the smart girls to answer his question, I desperately tried to purge the image of the flame-engulfed young martyr from my mind.

The lengthening silence pulled me sharply back to reality. Mother Bridget was rattling and crackling dangerously, the priest's brown eyes were staring dreamily off into space, and blue hair ribbons were moving all over the place.

Suddenly a headline from that morning's edition of the St. John's *Daily News* flashed into my mind. Totally out of character, I impulsively raised my hand. Mother Bridget, after her initial shock, despairingly turned her head to the wall and closed her eyes in weary resignation.

"Father! The name of the Prime Minister of Canada is Mackenzie King."

Every May ribbon in the room swirled in my direction. Mother Bridget, shocked, baffled and relieved, smiled and crackled happily. I looked straight into her surprised eyes and thought, *Fooled you! I can read*. I think she heard me.

Gratified, the young and handsome Canadian priest dipped into his pocket and called me forward. As a reward I was given a holy picture of the martyred girl. It depicted her surrounded by savage tormentors, flames licking around her heels, in the worst of her many sufferings. He patted my head in kind dismissal and I eagerly inhaled his sweet cologne and brushed against his sleeve with my hand.

I returned shakily to the last seat in the last row. My hard-won classroom anonymity was lost forever.

Two years later Newfoundland became the tenth province of Canada; my mother got the baby bonus and pretty well everyone in the school knew the name of the Canadian prime minister. Pink bubble gum appeared in the candy stores. No big deal, really, although the baby bonus made my mother happy, and consequently I survived my adolescence.

I spent the rest of that school year basking in newly acquired fame; suddenly upgraded to smart, I found myself dumped into one of the coveted front desks. The exposure made me nervous and I missed my pastoral view of the convent garden. At the end of the school year I was moved out of the B group forever and into the grade six A group, where I produced the odd noteworthy sentence and poem but barely bluffed my way through math.

Chapter 10

My mother often called me a "house devil and a street angel." The name was meant to keep me humble, I guess.

In my persona as "street angel" I was known to be a very reliable girl and an honest one.

If I was sent to do an errand, I could be counted on to return with the right goods and the correct change.

One morning, during my summer holidays, I was sitting on our front steps waiting for some of my friends to come out to play. I heard my name being called gently from across the street. I quickly jumped up and ran to the house where an elderly lady, Mrs. Cousins, was standing in the doorway. She was still wearing her housecoat. I knew her husband was ill because I had seen the doctor, with his little black bag, leave their house about five minutes earlier.

I stood before her eagerly, ready to do her errand and, I hoped, collect a few pennies for the job.

Sure enough, she needed my courier services.

"My darling, will you take this prescription to the drugstore and get it filled for me? Mister is awful sick and the doctor thinks this new medicine might help him to pick up a bit. Personally, I, myself, don't have much hope that it will do any good, but we have to try, don't we, my child? Now come back as soon as you can. I, myself, thinks that the poor bastard is at death's door and nothing at all will help him at this stage. I have a feeling and I'm never wrong. He'll be going today, so he will. Hurry up now, my love, won't you?"

She looked very distressed and quickly made the sign of the Cross over me before I took off down the street.

Getting the prescription filled and ready to go took the druggist about half an hour. I paid for it and ran out the door, the store bell clanging behind me.

I beat it back to the square and knocked as hard as I could on the front door. There was no answer.

Finally I heard her voice calling faintly from upstairs. I assumed she was in the bedroom with her dying husband. So I gently opened the door and ventured into the front hall. Suddenly Mrs. Cousins materialized at the top of the stairs and, with her finger to her lips, beckoned me.

Mr. Cousins lay in the bed, looking half gone. The blinds were pulled down in the bedroom. The walls were blanketed with pictures of various saints, each of them, I'm sure, in the mind of Mrs. Cousins, capable of curing her poor husband.

Above the bed was the inevitable framed picture of Christ, copious amounts of blood pouring unimpeded from His violated Sacred Heart.

A huge crucifix on a black metal stand rested on an intricate doily on one of the bureaus.

A small coal stove was pumping out ferocious bursts of hot air, even though the day outside was fairly mild and sunny. There was a pail of hot water on top of the stove, to take the dryness out of the air and help Mr. Cousins to breathe easier, I surmised.

I was shocked when I saw him. He was lying on his side, a shadow of his former self, with sweat pouring from his brow. He had been a big, hearty man the last time I had seen him walking up Allan Square. I agreed with his wife, it could very well be the last day he would spend in Allan Square.

She motioned me to sit in a chair a nice distance from the bed. I had not anticipated being invited into the sick room. Usually I simply delivered my message, collected my few coins and hightailed it to the candy store.

"Stay a little while, my child, won't you please? I don't

want to be alone with him. It frightens me, the thoughts of him going. We don't have a chick or a child; it's times like this a woman needs children.

"Perhaps you and I will say the rosary for him after I gives him this new medicine? Would you mind? A good little convent girl like you; sure, I knows ye won't mind staying, will you, my darling?"

I nodded like a good little convent girl.

There was silence in the room. Mrs. Cousins tiptoed away from the bed and stopped at my chair.

"I'm just going downstairs for a minute to call the Palace; you know, my child, where the Archbishop lives. I have to call and get a priest to come and give him the Last Rites."

She bustled out the door, and I was left with Mr. Cousins. He was clearly waiting for his end. Every now and then a deep cough caused his body to shake all over and he moaned in agony.

Then he began to call a name. I presumed he was calling for his wife. "Fan! Fan! Where are ye, Fan?"

She came bustling in the door, breathless from the stairs. I was so scared that I was holding my breath.

"The priest is on his way!" She spoke tenderly to her husband and held his hand.

Suddenly he sat bolt upright in the bed and put his hand on her shoulder.

"We had a good life together, didn't we, Fan? We had many a good time in this bed, maid, didn't we?"

Mrs. Cousins looked at me apologetically. I felt my face go red.

Mr. Cousins lowered his voice, and I strained my ears to hear him. It was none of my business, but I was only human.

"Can you let me see yours for one last time, Fan?"

Fan pulled up her skirt and yanked down her navy flannel underpants.

"Can I touch it Fan? One last time and then I can die happy."

She moved closer to the bed, and with a beautiful smile

on his face, he reached out his hand to touch "it." Then he fell back on the pillows, gone.

With that the priest came in through the bedroom door. He didn't look at Mrs. Cousins or even notice me. His attention was on the dear departed.

He said softly, "I see I'm too late."

He walked to the bed and gazed down at Mr. Cousins. Mrs. Cousins stood at his back and pulled up her drawers, and then smoothed her skirts down demurely.

Still gazing down at the corpse, the priest murmured gently, "Look at the smile on his face. He's a happy man. You can console yourself with that, Mrs. Cousins."

He then put on his stole and began to administer the Sacrament of Extreme Unction, as it was called when I was a kid.

Mrs. Cousins and I were both too shaken to attempt the rosary.

Chapter 11

Before the arrival of my stepfather on the scene, I don't recall hearing too much foul language floating around our place. The occasional "Jesus, Mary and Joseph! For Christ's sake! Cursed to hell's fiery flames!" and a few other similar oaths were common enough – nothing to really make anyone's hair stand on end. Nor was there a great deal of swearing in the streets among the kids. Each front door had its own set of ears and detailed reports would have been made, quickly and without mercy, to the families of the culprits. Then, as expected, all hell would break loose, and the informants would rest content, knowing that their civic duty had been done.

"It takes a village to raise a child" applied to Allan Square.

When my stepfather's Saturday night fights began in earnest, I suddenly began hearing words that were worthy of the worst tavern in town and the most infamous whorehouse. I didn't know it then, but those words were to have a profound effect on my psyche.

When things finally quieted down on the nights that he was drunk, as I was struggling to get some sleep the oaths ran through my head like some gruesome mantra, and they were still there the next morning. Some of the words I had never heard before and wondered what in God's name they had to do with my mother, at whom they were directed. Every filthy name that a man can shout at a woman was called down on her undeserving head.

She ran from him one night and stood petrified against my bedroom wall, with her fingers over her mouth to warn me not to say anything, and her terrified eyes staring. Even her ample share of guts had its limits. I watched from my bed as he found her, and I heard the crack as he backhanded her across the face.

I remember feeling, for the first but not the last time, the "flight or fight" syndrome – that sneaky precursor of panic disorder. Helplessly, I pulled my eyes away from my mother's face and yanked the blankets up over my head. I pretended there was no one in my room. Somehow that was what I knew she would want me to do, so that he wouldn't notice my presence and maybe turn his rage on me as well. But inside, where I lived, I really wanted to stick a knife in his back and twist it. Childhood rage is rarely, if ever, satisfied, and for that I am thankful, if unrepentant.

I told one of my friends on the street about his cursing and she promptly demonstrated her own swearing skills:

"Shit! Shag! Bugger! Damn! Bitch!"

I acted impressed, but I remember thinking at the time, *You're nowhere near, girl!*

I quickly emulated her, a feat of memory that should have been used on my multiplication tables.

She was suitably impressed, and then we did it in unison. To dazzle her, I reamed off a few of my stepfather's most choice swear words. She was shocked, and puzzled about their possible meanings. Later she said she had told her mother about my swearing. As a result of her passing on that information, she was not allowed to play with me anymore.

My youngest brother, Bob, dealt with the foul words in his own way. He began to have terrible nightmares in which he screamed out, in verbatim at the top of his voice, the filthy language that had lulled him to sleep. Every word of it spewed out freely. He also took to sleepwalking, right out the front door and up the street. We had to follow him and guide him, swearing, all the way back to the house – all this without waking him. The neighbours must have thought the inmates were running the asylum.

Every now and then, before I perfected my routine of calling the police, some of the neighbours, sick and tired of being sick and tired, took matters into their own hands and made the call.

Saturday nights, while we were waiting for him to get home, my mother had his dinner warming in the oven. Before it landed in the oven, and while it was still a pristine, well-prepared, nourishing meal, my mother and I systematically spit all over his food and then added an extra dollop of gravy, for camouflage and aesthetics.

We watched as he downed the meal with drunken gusto, and then we waited for the uproar. We had the small satisfaction of knowing that whatever else he was, he was by then infected with any mysterious germs we both might have carried. On Allan Square, that was probably a fine variety. I don't know about my mother, but I never felt even a twinge of guilt about doctoring his meal. He deserved it.

My mother told me to never, ever become a waitress.

On the nights that he was lucky enough to stay out of the lock-up, he usually fell into a stupor after the fight, sated with food and germs.

One Sunday morning he couldn't seem to drag himself from the bed, or even to lift his head. I was scared, but hopeful; maybe he was going to die! Then he began to shake violently, and suddenly the bed began to shake, moving up and down on its metal casters. It made an awful racket, and I wondered what the hell was going on now.

It was the beginning of the end of his drinking career. This was a full-blown case of the delirium tremens – better known as the DTs. It was terribly scary for anyone watching.

One particular Saturday night, before the DTs episode, he went out to a nightclub, without my mother, of course.

When I got up the next morning, it was plain to see that he had been in some sort of serious fracas. I guess he picked on someone his own size, for a change. Anyway, his jaw was all wired up, and when I looked at him I felt a rush of joy. I was so happy that my satisfaction must have shown on my face. Even now, all these years later, I believe he got what was coming to him and cannot feel a shred of pity.

As far as I was concerned, his wired-up jaw made for the start of one mighty fine day.

Before he was married to my mother, he had a bunch of cronies who were also his drinking buddies. Mom made a hard and fast rule. None of his drinking buddies were allowed to "darken the door" of our place. One night he was not at home, and one of his drinking friends had the temerity to knock on our front door. There he stood on the step, with a case of Haig Ale and a brown paper bag, obviously filled with liquor. The bottles were showing over the top of the bag.

Mom took one look and uttered a few choice words that had him staggering back down the street in short order. "And don't come back!" She slammed the door and marched me back into the kitchen. Unless his crony told him, my stepfather never heard about the visit. He didn't mention it, as far as I knew, and I knew just about everything that was going on in our place. My role as observer was one I took quite seriously. In other words, I was a nosy little bitch.

The musical visitors of my father's time no longer came. The only music now was from the radio, no more live performances, no spoons, no accordions, and no step dancers. Our outport relatives no longer stayed over during their visits to town. It was too dangerous for them; none of them cared for my stepfather.

The only regular visitors were my mother's sister and her husband who lived in St. John's. They were constant from the beginning to the end; they shared everything they had with us, God bless them both. We all loved them dearly.

In the course of his travels around town, my stepfather had many opportunities to pick up "hot" products from one or the other of his more shady cronies. My mother would have none of it. Any "hot" item that turned up in the house was quickly tossed out the front door, with no care as to where it landed or who picked it up.

"We don't learn from him. He learns from us!" She was right again. He soon learned not to bring home ill-gotten goods. It was entirely too much trouble and not worth the hassle it caused. He was beginning to feel cravings for a peaceful life, at last. My mother was winning.

Chapter 12

My mother had a charge account at Bowring Brothers store on Water Street.

One Christmas she decided to trust me to use it, and only because she had nobody else to do it.

"Now!" my mother declared decisively. "You're to go down to Bowring Brothers and do the Christmas shopping! Remember what I told you. Get in, get what you can, and then get out before they stop you!"

She decided that we would wait for the week leading up to Christmas Eve to do the shopping. Then all the stores would be really busy, blocked to the rafters with last-minute shoppers. Bowring's would be no different, she said. They'd be clogging the aisles, looking for last-minute bargains. I was expected to clog along with the best of them.

I remember beginning to feel a little queasy. An attack of nerves appeared as a familiar, torturous knotting in my stomach. I felt like the world's most evil and least-practiced kleptomaniac.

Of course, my mother noticed the sudden pallor of my face and immediately jumped at me.

"Now madam! Get that look off your face.There's nothing for you to be afraid of; you can do this. You're big enough and you're ugly enough! Or, would you rather see your brothers with nothing at all for Christmas? After all, they won't lock up a child during the Christmas season, and it's not as if you'll be stealing or anything! You'll be using my account, and I always pay my bill on time!"

My mother was not one to live on credit. She had only one charge account, and it was at Bowring Brothers. She used her account sparingly. She kept her little bit of cash in a Sucrets can. The can was kept under the cushion of her rocking chair. I guess that could be called sitting on your cash. Thinking about the size of that can, it's easy to figure there wasn't much cash floating around under her cushion. But still, there was always enough money in the can to pay her monthly bill at Bowring Brothers.

Only one time during the year did she get a little reckless with her account. That was at Christmas, and she wasn't really the one to go mad, even then. Instead, she drafted me into temporary insanity, bullying me into doing the shopping. I was given extra leeway in my "spending" in honour of the season.

Obviously a bit unsure of her account balance and her credit limit, she turned me into a virtual basket case while giving me instructions on how to deport myself when shopping in one of the biggest department stores in downtown St. John's.

First she prepared a list of items for my stepfather and each of my four brothers. I was to pick up brown leather Romeo slippers and a plaid shirt for the man of the house, and socks, gloves, ties, and shirts for my brothers. My mother's brother-in-law and her favourite sister were at the bottom of the list. They would each get a gift if my shopping spree were allowed to continue that far by whoever controlled the credit limits at Bowring Brothers. You could say my aunt and uncle were on the list on a contingency basis only. I figured there wasn't much hope gift-wise for either of them. I had some serious doubts about reaching the end of the list.

One of the rules of my shopping expedition was that I go alone; no friends were to accompany me. They might distract me from my purpose. Besides, my mother insisted, there was absolutely no need for the neighbours, or their brats, to know her business.

"Now, you listen to me carefully!" my mother continued

with her instructions. "This account is the same as money. Therefore, you spend it carefully. Get value for your dollar. Sale items are always the best! You're big enough and you're ugly enough to do this right."

"Big enough and ugly enough" was her favourite mantra for me. She used it frequently, and I had finally reached the point in my life where I believed it without question.

"Now, wash your face and hands and comb your hair. We can't have you going down to Bowring Brothers looking like a poor little streel! You never know who the hell you'll see down there, and I don't want you making a holy show out of us all."

Evening was just beginning to fall as I hightailed it out the door. Large, soft snowflakes glistened in the streetlights. Everything was beginning to look and feel very much like Christmas. I felt myself getting into the mood. My fear gradually lifted and was replaced with a sense of excitement and anticipation.

When I reached Water Street, the Mount Cashel Orphanage annual Christmas raffle was taking place in a building right next to Bowring Brothers store. Orphan boys were swinging huge bells to attract any and all comers.

The floor was covered with sawdust, tickets were being sold, raffle wheels were turning, winning numbers were shouted out, and an air of great excitement prevailed. I stood there for a while, feeling my own anticipation build. I even felt lucky, and if I'd had any spare cash I would have bought a ticket for myself in an attempt to win a Christmas turkey.

Instead I turned into Bowring Brothers and wandered around for a while, enjoying the Christmas decorations and the piped-in seasonal music. I lingered over items that I knew wouldn't stand a hope in hell of going on my mother's account. Her credit limit only extended so far, but I still enjoyed the looking.

I suddenly began to have the feeling that I was being shadowed. I stole a glimpse to my left side and spotted a seedy-looking man dressed in a long black overcoat. He was sizing me up, and I began to wonder if maybe he was a house detective or even something more sinister.

I was very precocious, although not street smart, and I was picking up some serious bad vibes from that guy. I moved away without acknowledging his interest. He sidled along on my tail. I was beginning to feel very nervous.

I wandered around and eventually picked up everything on the list, without being stopped by the real store detective or the CID. I really didn't know which would be worse, but the question appeared to be academic; nobody attempted to stop me at all. I was even able to get to the bottom of my mother's list, selecting a lovely set of wall plaques for my aunt and a pair of blue, red and white diamond socks for my uncle. My mother liked diamond socks; she thought they were classy. The sleazy man was still on my tail.

Just before I was ready to finish my shopping, I noticed a display of snuggies, my mother's favourite undergarments. On impulse, since my shopping had so far been unimpeded, I decided to get my mother a vest and a pair of underpants in pink; then I really got carried away and picked up another set for her in blue.

By this time I was in the cash line, and the man was sticking to me like Super Glue.

I watched the little metal cylinders the sales clerks used to send the bills and the cash to the office. I waited until the woman in front of me received her change by way of return cylinder and was toddling her way toward the door.

By this time his hands had gotten busy and I could feel one of them caressing my leg. Up, down, then in little circles. I began to feel very sleepy. Then I felt his hand withdraw, and he began a soft whistle, maybe his idea of a lullaby. The sales clerk smiled at me kindly, and in no time at all the transaction was complete and I made it out the door, laden with Christmas shopping.

I was so scared that I didn't even look back to see if he was following me. The leg he had been caressing was burning as if the hand was still on it. I began to realize that

I had *liked* it when he touched me. I yearned for the nightly Act of Contrition and subsequent release from sin.

I belted it across the street like a bat out of hell. I ran on the double up the steep concrete steps leading to Bates Hill. I still didn't look back as I took Bates Hill to Theatre Hill. All the hills were doing nothing for my breathing. I was panting and gasping as I stole a quick look behind. My heart was beating fast, like an out-of-tune drum.

I hit number eight Allan Square, yanked open the door and slammed it behind me viciously.

I knew I had done well for my mother; her list was complete, she should be content. I was, however, more than a little worried about her reaction to the unauthorized purchase of her snuggies.

She was thrilled with my shopping on the whole. She balked a little at her new underwear but caved in quickly. She was indeed in dire need of new snuggies.

"Now madam! What's in that bag you're hiding behind your back?"

I handed her the bag without saying a word. She opened it and nearly hit the ceiling.

"Why you little Antichrist!" She reached out to clout me but I nimbly evaded her.

"You've got a nerve like a bloody toothache, that's what you've got! I've half a mind to send you back with them. That's what I should do, if I had any sense at all. What do I need with two new pairs of snuggies!"

Then she finally noticed my burning face and asked what was the matter with me.

I told her about the fondling man, but I didn't mention the fact that I had liked it.

She shook her head and then held it in her hands.

"Sweet Christ, girl! You haven't got the sense God gave a calf! You're not safe to be let out alone. Why didn't you call for help or else pound the shit out of him and scream your head off?"

I crawled into bed, said an Act of Contrition in which I literally begged forgiveness for breathing and for buying the extra snuggies set for my poor mother's cold bum. Mostly, though, I expressed repentance for liking "it"!

Although I hadn't cribbed a thing for myself, I felt strangely content and drifted off to sleep peacefully with my fondled leg still burning comfortingly.

I decided that I must be starved for affection. Merry Christmas! It was a great but frightening night at Bowring Brothers.

Chapter 13

Allowance money was in very short supply in our house. In fact, around our place the word "allowance" was not in common usage. Every Saturday, however, in return for scrubbing the flat, I did get a dime. This dime was invariably used for the movies. That's what it cost to get into the theatre in those days.

A dime a week just did not cut it, as far as my friend Moll and I were concerned. So we took to checking under the seats of the theatre, after the show, to see if any unfortunate had dropped loose change from pocket or purse. We sometimes found enough for a few candies or a chocolate bar. We had no pride to speak of, and we didn't really care who saw us. The searching under the seats wasn't really rewarding. It was the original non-profit organization, as far as we were concerned.

Moll and I talked it over and came up with what we were sure would be a suitable alternative to the hit-and-miss one we had been using so much energy on, all that bending and crawling over the hard theatre floor and trying to duck the ushers.

Eureka! We thought of the Americans. There seemed to be millions of Yanks stationed at Fort Pepperrell, the US Base bordering on Quidi Vidi Lake. They asked girls out on dates, and they often went to movies. Where else was there to go? Everyone knew they were all filthy rich and that their roads back in the States were paved with gold. *They* would be our new source of income, Moll and I finally decided.

Our first bit of research involved staking out the lineups at the various theatres. The Nickel, the Paramount and the Capitol were the three in our immediate neighbourhood. Our second problem was the chance of being caught. We dismissed the unknown consequences as being of little importance and before we knew it, we were in business.

The lineups were always good, two people in each row, always a couple. Most of the men wore the uniform of the US. To us, that spelled money. We avoided anyone who didn't look like a Yank as if he was carrying the plague. It was dicey, exciting and definitely scary.

Moll and I always started at the back of the lineup. We worried about losing income from those in the front, but there was really no choice. We couldn't risk being caught by any of the ushers or the management. God only knew where that might lead.

"Hello, mister, can you spare a dime or a nickel?" We never asked for anything larger; we weren't greedy, simply deprived and hungry.

Usually the gent was forthcoming and the girlfriend's head turned away in shame at two of her fellow citizens being so young and brazen! God help us. The Yank usually fished into his pants pocket and pulled out a few coins, which he handed to us with a smile. We were always very appreciative and extremely polite. We were not attending convent schools for nothing, after all. We had a little couth; not much, mind you, just enough to let us scrape by.

We worked our way up to the fifth couple from the start of the lineup before we slithered away into the night. Sometimes we wound up with two or three dollars each, a veritable fortune in our eyes.

I don't remember when or why we stopped our bumming. In my memory the begging-for-money interlude is there and then suddenly it's gone. Just like that. I've talked to Moll, my co-bummer, who is now a Yank herself, having married one and moved to the States. She doesn't know when we stopped bumming or why. She does fondly remember our visits to the lineups, though, and even recollects spending the cash. She told me that one of the neighbourhood girls accused us of teaching her how to bum at the theatres. She and I scoffed at that. There's no way we would have wanted anyone else to cut in on our territory; there were barely enough coins for the two of us. So if the other kid bummed, she did it under her own power. That's our story and we're sticking to it!

Going to the movies was always a great bit of fun, and we soon devised a scheme to make it even more enjoyable. We managed to get ourselves smuggled in by a few sympathetic ushers. They only wanted a few kisses in return and we gladly complied, considering it a fair exchange, and wondering at the same time why anybody would be foolish enough to want to kiss the two of us. We had not yet realized our developing powers as young women.

I can see them now, the ushers, God love them, looking young and handsome in their braided uniforms. It was almost like having your very own Yank. The ushers soon tired of our kisses, though, and called us babies when we refused to French kiss. After a suitable period of mourning, we selected new ushers to share a few kisses in return for free admittance. God knows where it all might have ended.

As with all my shady doings, the memory of when this one ended has faded from my mind. To quote Dickens, "It was the best of times, it was the worst of times."

There was another boon attached to going to the movies. Many of the boys collected comic books and brought them to the movies for trading. Moll and I had no comics to trade, but we desperately wanted to get some. So, we decided to trade kisses in exchange for comics. We laid down the rules to the boys right up front: one kiss for one comic, and definitely no tongue. We thought that was a fairly good deal. Who else would kiss some of them, anyway? This was how we consoled our Catholic consciences, whenever they threatened to stir. Besides, there was always the nightly Act of Contrition.

We wound up with a fine collection of comic books and, as far as we knew, our reputations remained fairly intact.

We were certain that our transgressions were all forgiven. If not during nightly prayers, then we were certainly purified through weekly confessions. I hated confession with a passion.That little box reminded me very unpleasantly of the coal pound. There were no rats or mice there, but then I didn't know that for sure, did I?

Our kissing experiments didn't end with the movies and the comic books. There remained the Kirk – St. Andrews Presbyterian Church. We never called the church grounds off Long's Hill anything but the Kirk. It was one of our playgrounds during summer holidays. The grass was long and unkempt and the grounds were really a huge hill. We loved rolling down that hill.

There was supposed to be an old graveyard buried under the grass. It makes sense – churchyard, graveyard. It didn't stop us from playing kissing games with any boys who happened to be available. One day three of the girls from our neighbourhood, including Moll and me, happened to be up at the Kirk when we decided it was time to discover which of us was growing pubic hair and how that hair was coming along. I remember Moll and I were the losers. So all the kissing really had no effect on the growth of pubic hair.

We already knew that anyway! Besides, we were only beaten by one.

Chapter 14

In the meantime, my strange visits to the dead continued. My mother never caught on to the fact that I had visited wakes regularly. The only ones she knew about were the "duty" ones, the ones I attended in her place and offered the sympathy of our family along with a Mass card.

This was during the time when all wakes were held at home and people spent shifts keeping their loved one company for three days, some of them getting stoned drunk and breaking out in song after a suitable period of mourning. I saw no booze at any of the wakes I attended. But then again, I wasn't interested in the liquor, just the food.

I guess I was about twelve years old when my fascination with the dead took a new and probably more emotionally healthy turn. (If any of my children had shown this same propensity for the rituals of death I would have been horrified, but then again, I lived in a different time and place when I was a kid.)

My father's family had been involved in the undertaking business, so maybe it was in my blood. Dad used to take us when we were small to visit the place where they built the caskets and prepared the body for its final ride. My brother Jerry remembered visiting one day and being told by a cousin to get into one of the boxes for a rest. Jerry, in his innocence, did attempt to do just that. When he opened the box, there was a body lying there, all dressed up and ready to go. It traumatized him to no end, and he didn't forget it to his dying day.

As a matter of fact, the branch of Dad's family with the undertaking business made the arrangements for Dad's funeral. I remember one of them had a car, and he took me for an ice cream cone.

When I got back home, my father's casket was gone, and so were my brothers Jerry and Lew. They were walking in the funeral procession behind the horse-drawn hearse to the big church on Military Road. And later they would walk to Mount Carmel Cemetery. My mother was at home; in those days women did not walk in a funeral procession, and few people had cars.

Maybe I didn't feel that my period of mourning for my father had been complete, and that's why, apart from the hunger, I was drawn to wakes. Who knows? My fascination was soon to end, and my status as a professional mourner came to an abrupt halt.

It took only two more wakes to shake me out of my peculiar need to be near the dead and their mourners.

One of the wakes was a "duty" wake; we knew the family, and the mother had died. I remember walking down Theatre Hill, knocking on the door and being led into the room where the casket lay. I nearly passed out in shock! Cradled in the crook of the mother's arms lay a baby, as tiny and perfect as a little doll. I had had no warning there was a baby involved. It was one of the saddest sights of my young life, and I have not seen anything like it since. I nearly died with the pain of it all. With that wake I began to feel a decided distaste for melancholy and all things related to it.

The wake that really clinched the deal, though, and turned me completely from my strange addiction was something else again!

At this particular viewing I had given my condolences to a member of the family and then knelt by the casket to pay my respects to the deceased, an elderly woman. I took in her pale blue dress, her necklace, her rings, her beautiful snow-white hair, and the lovely blue rosary beads with a silver Cross entwined around her tiny hands. I then took a seat and sized up the one remaining mourner. It was a man and he looked supremely bored, sitting in the room with a young stranger whom nobody had been able to identify. Suddenly he got up and went out into the hall and toward the kitchen. I was left alone with the corpse.

The noise started out as a tiny rattle. Probably nobody but me was able to hear it. I realized that the rattle was coming from the direction of the casket. My blood ran cold. I was terrified as the rattle became louder and more frenzied. I looked at the casket without moving from my seat across the room. I never did like to sit too close to a casket.

The next thing I knew, the hands of the deceased were moving above the level of the sides of the casket. I was frozen in place and breathing heavily. It was almost as bad as the excursions to the coal pound. I was struggling to catch my breath when, suddenly, the beautiful blue rosary came flying across the room, barely missing my head.

I could almost hear her: "Fly to hell's flames, you saucy little brat! Who the hell are you anyway? We don't know you! I never laid eyes on you in my life before. Get the hell out of my wake. Go!"

I looked at the beautiful rosary beads crumpled at my feet just as the commotion was starting in the kitchen.

A woman's voice yelled, "Jesus, Mary and Joseph! What in the name of Christ was that racket?"

The family came crashing down the hall just as I was making my way out the front door.

"Mother!" they were screaming at the body.

"Where's her rosary beads?" they asked each other.

"My God! Look! They're on the floor!"

"What happened to that little one who was here? Where did she go?"

"Somebody get her and find out what the hell happened here!"

"Who was she anyway?"

It was too late for them to catch me. I could run when I had to. In what seemed like no time at all, I was down Queen's Road, up Allan Square and into the house.

When I closed the door behind me I was shaking like a leaf. My mother said my face was as white as a sheet and she asked what the devil was wrong.

I told her a big black dog had chased me.

The nightmares lasted for months and they were not about a big black dog. For a while I took a different route to school to avoid passing the house of the "Flying Rosary." Word got around the neighbourhood about the strange story of the rosary beads. The undertaker attributed the moving hands to some problem with embalming. Enough said.

My days as a professional mourner were well and truly finished. From that wake on I attended them only as a duty, when forced to do so by my mother.

Chapter 15

Now that I was unable to satisfy my strange longings to be around the dead and their mourners, I was forced to find alternative entertainment.

I began to drop into various houses in the neighbourhood where it was known there was basically an open door policy. In other words, they liked visitors and welcomed them.

My friends and I went into another girl's vestibule and played pick-up sticks or some other mindless game that kept us occupied for about half an hour.

Then I straggled home only to be verbally assaulted by my mother for seeking refuge and company in a strange house.

"And tell me, madam, just what is wrong with your own home that you'd rather be anywhere else? Do you know what you are, missy? You're a cabin hunter, that's what you are!"

She let me have it with the wet wash towel, scoring a direct hit against my left ear. The blow sent me spinning across the room, screaming that I had gone deaf and would never recover my hearing.

She was not unduly worried and demanded, looking for another victim, "Where is your brother Bobby?"

The next day my mother cornered Bob and demanded to know where he had been the night before. Bob exhibited no fear and came right out and told the truth.

"I was up Long's Hill at the Kellys' place. We were listening to the radio, playing cards and talking. Oh, and eating. Mrs. Kelly had made some bread and she fried some up for toutons. They were some good, too, with a cup of tea. Then I fell asleep and they put a blanket over me and I stayed the night!"

Mr. Kelly was Mom's cousin from Tickle Cove, and he had very strongly disapproved of her marrying my stepfather. I was listening to this exchange between Bob and Mom with interest. I wondered why Bob had not yet received a clout across the head.

Without any more fuss he hit the bedroom and flopped into one of the beds.

His days as a cabin hunter were allowed to continue with barely a blip in between visits. When my mother asked him why he spent so much time at the Kelly place he answered simply, "Because they treat me better up there, and the food is better, too!"

"Now!" she said. "They're going to pump him within an inch of his life, and he's going to spill his guts like a prisoner being interrogated in the war. He'll do it for a lousy piece of cake, for Christ's sake."

So Bob continued to cabin hunt at the Kelly house and grew plump and healthy-looking. From that time on, he was almost like a double agent.

He was interrogated at the Kellys' place, and then when he ventured home, Mom gave him the third degree. Each household soon knew exactly what was going on in the other one, and Bob was feeding Mom some mighty tidy morsels. God alone knew what intelligence he was passing along to the Kellys.

My experiment in cabin hunting was brought to an immediate halt, though. My mother grabbed me by the hair and forced my face up to hers,"Your cabin hunter days are finished, do you hear me? Finished! I wouldn't trust you any farther than I can throw you. You'll be leaking no news out of this house, madam!"

I deeply regretted this turn of events. There were so many cabins, so much news to be spread. From then on, when my mother asked me if I had any news, she found that I never had anything worth sharing. So she concentrated on Bob and his lovely loose tongue. I was off the hook.

I took to going to the Gosling Memorial Library, the biggest cabin in town. As a matter of fact, it was a cabin hunter's paradise. When my mother asked me who I'd seen at the library, she got no info from me. I'd simply say, "Nobody!" My lips were sealed – it was Mom's loss.

Chapter 16

My stepfather was not the only man on Allan Square who, because of alcohol, turned the street upside down every Saturday night. He was, however, the most violent and the loudest.

Another neighbourhood man from Livingstone Street who liked his drink staggered home regularly and, as far as we knew, quietly lay down to sleep or was knocked down by his very aggressive wife.

If he was not home by nine, she could be seen, as regular as the clock, purposefully striding down Allan Square in her printed housedress, broom at the ready, to Dynamite Dunne's tavern on Theatre Hill. Fortunately for this gutsy wife, the bar was just around the corner from Allan Square, within easy walking distance. Within ten minutes – we figured that was the minimum time he could fight her off – up the street they'd come, himself staggering from one side of the sidewalk to the other, his much smaller and wiry wife prodding him from behind with her broom. It was funny!

When the door closed behind them, we didn't hear another peep for the rest of the night. The Black Maria never made a stop at their house. The wife was the power there. She did her own policing, and she did it extremely well. Mister was under her control to a large degree, but he had managed to override his fear enough to go into the tavern in the first place, which said a great deal about the strength of his cravings for a few drinks and a bit of peace.

My stepfather's drinking haunt was not on Theatre Hill.

His favoured watering hole was at the Ritz Tavern, which was on New Gower Street, almost at the corner of Adelaide Street. In those times it was quite common to see men staggering along New Gower Street, day and night, east and west, to their homes. Drunken men, stray dogs and the odd prostitute loved the area and kept it hopping. At least it could be said that the men didn't drink and drive, although this was not strictly a matter of choice.

Only the very well off had their own vehicles, and they definitely did not frequent the Ritz. The rest of them, the riffraff, as my mother liked to say, had to use shank's mare – which meant their legs, under their own power, such as what power remained at the end of an evening at the Ritz. The odd big spender arrived home in a taxi, usually a Gulliver's cab. My stepfather never did reach that point in his drinking career; he invariably arrived home via shank's mare.

Looking back on it now, it seems to me it must have been a very slow stagger up Theatre Hill for him. One step forward and two steps back at the very best.

One particular Saturday night, ten o'clock came and he still had not darkened the door. My mother was getting very edgy, wanting to get the racket over and done with at a decent time so that the neighbours would not be disturbed.

My cousin Bernadette was staying with us at the time, for a short while, sleeping with me on the little folding cot in my room. There wasn't space to sleep side by side, so she slept at one end of the bed and I slept at the other. We were both tall girls. Neither of us had room to turn our bodies. We fought all night long in a futile attempt to keep pungent feet out of each other's faces.

"Now where the devil is that bastard? I suppose he's not lying on the street somewhere, making a holy show out of us!" My mother was getting worried.

"There'll be nothing holy about the show he's making!" I whispered to Bernadette.

She nodded sagely. Although unused to such behaviour from her own father at home, she had seen my stepfather in action a few times, and she knew what was coming.

The light bulbs were going on over my mother's head as she eyed Bernadette and me.

Finally she made her decision.

"Now ye two! What I wants ye to do is walk down to the Ritz and take a look to see if he's in there! Don't go looking so frightened. Ye're both big enough and ugly enough to take care of yourselves. Sure, who'd want either of ye, anyway?"

Bernadette was horrified at being called ugly by her aunt and answered her back. "Plenty of them in the Ritz would want us, that's who!"

The "big enough and ugly enough" part had rolled off me like water off a duck's back. I said nothing, knowing that resistance to Mom was futile.

"Ye're not to go into the Ritz, ye foolish things! Just look in, take a look, that's all I wants ye to do!"

"Sweet Jesus, Mary and Joseph!" Bernadette stormed as we walked down Allan Square.

Just before we turned the corner at the bottom of the street, I looked back and saw Mom watching us from the front door. She waved an arm, urging us to keep going, and keep going we did.

Once on New Gower Street, we smelled the stale liquor even before we reached the tavern. We could see the blue-grey haze of cigarette smoke drifting out the opened door, filtering through the dim light, and we could hear the raucous sound of men's voices.

"Sweet Christ!" Bernadette whispered. "Me mudder would skin me alive, so she would, if she knew I was doing this! Let's go back!"

I whispered, "Don't be so foolish, girl. What do ya think Mom will do to us if we go back? She'll have our guts for garters!"

We reached the door of the tavern and peered inside. Nobody seemed to notice us. We might as well have been invisible for all the attention we received. That suited us just fine, so we forgot Mom's orders and ventured inside. We had to – we couldn't see our hands in front of us, for all the smoke, let alone pick out any particular drunk.

We walked up and down the place; my cousin took one side and I took the other. There were booths on each side, and we peered intently into each one. There was no sign of His Lordship in that tavern, but it sure was crowded and noisy. He might have taken a washroom break, for all we knew, but we had had enough and left the dust of the place behind us. Our nerves were shot! We weren't even worried about what Mom would do when we got home.

On the way home we discussed what she had expected us to do anyway if he had been there. Carry him home on our backs? Or link into him and drag him up Theatre Hill?

Mom was lying asleep on her bed when we got back, exhausted from worry and nerves. There was no sign of him.

Bernadette and I collapsed on the little folding cot and, our dreams polluted with the smell of stale beer and cigarette smoke, proceeded to go to sleep and to launch our nightly battle for relief from poking feet.

I have no idea when he got home, but he was there in the morning when we got up.

Chapter 17

After my stepfather's earlier Sunday morning bout of the DTs, he was suddenly gone from the house. Either they took him away by ambulance or he left under his own steam, but he was gone, for about three or four months. I found out later that he had been in the mental hospital, taking the "cure."

One evening a doctor came to the door and went with Mom into the front room. He asked her if she would take her husband back and give him a second chance. He assured her that my stepfather was indeed a changed man. Somehow or other, with my usual sleight of hand, I had managed to slip into the room behind the doctor and to escape my mother's notice.

"No!" I screamed. "Don't take him back. Don't take him back! We don't need him."

She simply ignored me and, of course, she took him back.

When he returned to the fold, he was good as his word and never had a drink after the mysterious treatments, until after my mother passed away.

Saturday nights became fairly tranquil, no more visits from the police and the Black Maria.

Our place quickly became almost respectable and fairly normal. Mom and I had no reason anymore to spit on his food. So he was relatively safe from strange germs. As far as my mother was concerned, we had never done that in the first place anyway. How about that! I would swear on a stack of bibles that we did.

When my stepfather was friends with my father, he had the reputation of stealing all of Dad's girlfriends, so my mother was the one he didn't get to meet until after she was safely married to Dad. My stepfather must have hated to let such a pretty one get away, but, son of a gun! He did wind up getting her in the end. Life is sure kind of strange in a funny way.

After he stopped drinking, he stopped the foaming at the mouth and fighting, and of course he stopped tossing the furniture around. We had to buy new dishes, because almost all the ones we had earlier had been broken.

My mother was not a woman to revisit her past, especially the unhappy parts. I guess that was good, but it did not satisfy the hunger and need I had to hear stories about my father. Nobody in our house talked about him, but I did know we all missed him sorely. I later knew that he never really left us. I have felt his presence all my life.

Mom also did not backbite, saying that, "People in glass houses should not throw stones." So if an unmarried girl we knew became pregnant, that fact would never pass my mother's lips. I remember noticing and being impressed by this character trait of hers. It was a rare one on Allan Square, which was a veritable hive of gossip.

On Saturday nights, instead of coming home with a load in, my stepfather began to bring presents for Mom. He brought nylons, not one pair but five or ten pairs at a time. He brought Pot of Gold chocolates and fruit. I suppose he was trying to make up for lost time. Mom had to hide the chocolates from me. She said it was because my teeth were beginning to rot, but I had my doubts, although the teeth were indeed rotting, slowly but surely. It was very traumatic for me to watch it happening, and there was no such thing as going to the dentist for fillings. Also, I had two fangs growing down over my front teeth.

My mother's words, which she repeated often – "You're big enough and ugly enough" – were really beginning to take root and leave a deep impression on me.

Then my stepfather bought a car. It was black and had a running board. I was really impressed. Just about every

Sunday afternoon, he'd take me and Mom for a drive out to what was then called the "country." We went in over Topsail Road to Holyrood and back home. It was a lovely long drive. We always stopped for an ice cream. These were the times when I felt almost like a normal kid.

My mother was delicate and not capable of heavy work. The doctor said that she'd had too many children for her constitution. She'd had rheumatic fever when she was young, and that had left her heart weakened, although nobody knew that at the time. She could not scrub the floors, and so I had been doing it since I was old enough to hold a scrubbing brush. I absolutely hated it! My brother Jack came home one time when I was on my knees scrubbing the hall, and he kicked over the whole bloody bucket of dirty water. I was wounded; I had not said or done anything to provoke such a mean act. I didn't speak to him for a week. He didn't seem to give a tinker's damn.

To my surprise, my stepfather suddenly decided to take over the scrubbing of the floors. He also took over what had been another job of mine, washing the dishes. Washing the dishes was not as easy as it sounded. First the water had to be brought to the kitchen from the cold water tap in the lobby and heated on the kitchen stove. Then the dishes had to be washed, rinsed, dried, and put away. It was a two-hour boring job, and I was delighted to be rid of it.

Within a short time, I was forced to take another look at my stepfather, seeing him in the unlikely role of family protector. It involved my brother Jack, who must have been about twelve at the time – I was eleven.

Jack had been having some trouble with a kid who lived up around the corner on Livingstone Street. The two boys were well-matched in size and could probably have handled their fights quite well on their own, but the father of the family, Mr. Peters, usually came out of his house and gave Jack a good tongue-lashing, effectively stopping the fisticuffs, frightening the daylights out of my brother in the process and declaring his son, in front of the neighbourhood kids, as the winner by default.

This caused Jack to lose face. I'm sure he didn't like it at all.

I suppose he must have told our stepfather, who really hadn't had a good fight since he gave up drinking and who suddenly saw the possibility of one at hand. When my stepfather had finally gotten tired of being arrested every Saturday night and gave up his drinking, Allan Square became a quieter, more peaceful place for the decent people who lived there. I enjoyed holding my head up instead of slinking shamefacedly out the front door after a night of his disgraceful behaviour.

One day, before we knew what was happening, he was out the door, still wearing his leather Romeo slippers, and off he charged, at a brisk pace, up Allan Square. Jack and I, along with a horde of neighbourhood kids, all of them smelling blood, followed close on his heels. I have to admit that I can still feel the sense of excitement, and even a strange bit of pride. Jack had someone to take up for him, someone grown-up. The bigger brothers were pretty good at protection, too, but I had never heard them ream off an oath like my stepfather could. I had a feeling that Mr. Peters and his little brat were soon going to hear some choice curse words.

My stepfather stopped before their front door and dragged his braces, which had been hanging down his pants, up over his shoulders.

He then pushed up the sleeves of his long johns shirt. There was not a sound from the kids who were waiting expectantly for the start of the action. Jack stood behind our stepfather, at a safe distance from the front door. I stood far enough away to be able to pretend I was not with them and close enough to see any action.

My stepfather banged on the door with enough force to put the fear of God into the hearts of those inside. I saw the lace curtains in the front window shake as someone took a quick glance at the rabble outside.

Mr. Peters, I must admit, had the courage to open the door and try to stare down our stepfather, whose face, by this time, had turned blood red with rage. He was truly a frightening sight. He opened his mouth, and every oath he knew came rushing out like an unending spew of vomit. He did not, however, as he had done during his drinking rages, foam at the mouth. I was glad of that; it would have spoiled the effect. Mr. Peters was warned not to approach Jack again or he would be arrested and charged with harassment.

Mr. Peters did not dignify the tirade with a response but grabbed his son by the scruff of the neck and dragged him inside.

The door slammed in our faces. Jack stood there with his fists clenched, at the ready, a satisfied smile on his face.

Mr. Peters' son was not allowed to play with our Jack anymore. Our stepfather began to teach Jack the rudiments of fixing cars.

Chapter 18

At Presentation Convent, the girls all wore uniforms. Navy blue serge dresses with black buttons to the waist, white collars and cuffs and black shoes and stockings. Everyone wore navy blue flannel bloomers. They were nice and warm. We had "gaiter" bags in the bad weather, for our rain boots or winter boots. The bags had drawstrings and were hung in the cloakroom with our coats.

My uniforms were always lovely, made with the best serge the Newfoundland government could supply. My mother had a cousin who worked at the penitentiary as a warden. His old uniforms were passed down to me. A seamstress who lived on Theatre Hill turned the material inside out, took my measurements, and turned out a brand new uniform each year. She also made two sets of collars and cuffs and trimmed them with lace.

The girls at Mercy Convent wore the same uniform, only their buttons were white and went from the neck down the dress to the hem. The white buttons usually meant money in the family, because the Mercy sisters catered to the daughters of the well-to-do.

At Presentation Convent the fees were called "coal fees" – hopefully enough to pay the heating bills for the school. I never paid a coal fee in my school life, and I was never asked to pay, probably because of my father's death at the beginning of my school career. Except for one experience in grade six, I was never made to feel like a charity case. I certainly received as good an education as the girls whose parents paid the "coal fees."

By the time I hit grade six, after getting out of the grade five B class, my second teeth were really starting to rot and I felt very embarrassed by that. I brushed them and brushed them with baking soda, but to no avail. There was no such thing as going to the dentist, not in our family, anyway. However, in spite of the rotting teeth, I still held my own in my studies and simply tried to avoid smiling. If something really struck my funny bone, I covered my mouth when it finally broke me up.

The move to the grade six A class meant a physical move to a new building as well. We were sent to the B.I.S. building. The initials stood for "Benevolent Irish Society" and our entrance was on Military Road across from the cathedral. "The closer to confession, my dear."

The B.I.S. property now contains very posh condos – imagine that!

The spirits of the very cowed convent girls probably slink along the halls every now and then, fleeting patches of navy blue and white, all of them trying in vain to find the right exit.

The teacher of the grade six A class, Sister Edward, was not one of my favourites. She was tall and slim, and when she smiled her face lit up. She never smiled at me and, of course, I never smiled at anyone, so we were even in that sense.

One particular morning she made my blood run cold with fear when she called me into the hall shortly after morning prayers, before class began. In the silent hall, outside the classroom door, she pointed to the floor. I thought she wanted me to kneel, but when I looked down, I saw a bucket and cleaning supplies – scrubbing brush, soap, cloths, etc. There was no mop, so obviously this was to be a kneeling job, and it was for me. I was puzzled, but at Presentation you didn't ask questions, just blindly obeyed.

I followed Sister Edward down the long hall, past closed classroom doors. I listened to her rosary beads clicking and watched her long, black skirt as it swished along the floor. I was carrying the cleaning materials and the bucket.

Finally she stopped before a door I had never noticed before. It didn't have the little window in the door, about halfway up, like the ordinary classroom doors did. This, I remember thinking, was probably her idea of solitary confinement. I was a little slow on the uptake that day. The pail and supplies would have been sufficient clues for another, less trusting girl.

She then took a ring of keys from her pocket, selected the correct one and turned the lock, all this without uttering a word, the bitch! Once inside the washroom I was informed, quite sternly, of the proper way to clean and disinfect a nun's washroom and of the standards of cleanliness demanded by the sisters.

She ordered me to fill the pail and go to my knees, ready for my toil. I heard the click of the key as she locked the door behind her. I was suddenly overcome with a black claustrophobia, reminiscent of my sojourns in the infamous coal pound on Allan Square.

But at least she hadn't turned off the light. I was locked in, but this was really a far cry from the coal pound, the obvious difference being that there was no coal, and also no rats or mice, or whatever they had been.

There was also no comparison to the washroom in our hall on Allan Square. This washroom was clean. As a matter of fact, it was spotless, and right then and there I figured that cleaning it would be as easy as hops. I was looking forward to it.

I put the toilet seat down and sat ruminating over the reason I had been given this particular assignment. I had no delusions that my selection was an honour; on the contrary, it was the meanest assignment she could have selected. I absolutely hated her then! She had made a holy show of me.

But the washroom itself was not daunting. I could have blown away the dust, and I seriously thought about doing just that, but fear held me back.

I started cleaning the toilet and the sink, slopping out the water with a vengeance. She may have thought that I wouldn't have a clue about cleaning floors, but she was wrong. I was young, but I had scrubbed many a floor in my day.

Every time I squeezed the scrubbing cloth, it was her skinny neck I was squeezing. Every turn of the scrubbing brush I made slammed into her crooked-looking face. The smell of Jeyes Fluid and Sunlight soap was heavy in the air. It was such a confined area, and the window wouldn't open. In spite of my near-asphyxiation, after a while I began to actually enjoy myself. It was so peaceful there. The washroom was finished in short order, and it was sparkling. I sat on the floor, crossed my legs and began reciting poems to myself. Once my hurt pride began to fade, it actually was a very enjoyable little break from class, and even at that point in my life I had the happy ability to bloom where I was planted.

I laid my head against the wall and began to drift off. I dreamed I was kicking Sister Edward's ass as she was scrubbing the washroom floor.

The next thing I knew, I heard the turn of the key in the lock. I scrambled up from the floor and gazed at the opening door warily. I had no watch, and so I had no idea at all of how much time had elapsed. My stomach, ever reliable, was making some rumbling noises, though, so I figured it was getting near lunchtime.

She came in and, with a swirl of her skirt, began her inspection: windows, window ledges, the cupboard under the sink and the toilet seat. It seemed as if she went over every inch of that floor. Then she stood there and simply stared at me, as if she was expecting me to say something, anything!

I said nothing that she could hear. But I was letting it all out inside, in some of my stepfather's finest oaths. "You big stupid bitch! Why don't you scrub your own fucking floor? You're big enough and you're ugly enough!"

My mother's description of me, which I had heard so many times, seemed made to order for Sister Edward.

"Fuck you, slut!" I finished my internal tirade with great relish. If I had been foolish enough to say any of this out loud, I would surely have been confined to the mental hospital.

She looked at me strangely, but she never said a word, simply opened the door and gestured me out. Then, with a pointing hand she ordered me back into the washroom to get the pail and other cleaning supplies.

I obediently picked everything up and trotted along the hall to the storeroom where the supplies were kept. I laid them gently on the floor and stood back respectfully, waiting for her to lock the door.

I practically skipped by her side down the quiet halls. I was really happy to get out from behind that locked door. All the while, the worst of my stepfather's drunken vocabulary raced around inside my head. I was actually scared that I would start foaming at the mouth. My rage was visceral, but carefully controlled.

Not a word was exchanged between Sister Edward and me as we returned to the classroom. Not a word of praise from her for a job well done, not a word of criticism.

The class was just getting ready to break for lunch when we got back from my period of enforced servitude. Every head turned when we entered the classroom. I kept my head down as I slid into my seat.

The class filed silently past her on the way out. I looked her right in the eye and silently brought down another oath on her head.

"Fly to hell's fiery flames, you wicked bitch! Fuck you! I'm no charity case!"

I ran down Queen's Road home to Allan Square, non-stop.

I did not tell my mother how I had spent my morning. She probably would have been proud that her girl had been singled out for such an honour. After all, not just anybody got to enter the inner sanctum of the nuns' washroom.

When I thought about it, I began to chuckle at the thought of those long, black skirts being hoisted before the process of elimination began.

I hadn't even known nuns used the washroom.

Chapter 19

One of the nicest surprises I received in my childhood was a present from my father's sister, my aunt Hann in New York. I don't remember how old I was, probably eleven.

It was a large box, and when I opened it I was absolutely thrilled. Inside were a new coat, hat and shiny black shoes. The coat was burgundy, and it had a black fur collar; the burgundy hat was trimmed with the same fur. When I took the coat out of the box, I was immediately disappointed. I knew at first glance that it would not fit. I tried it on anyway. It turned out to be way too small.

When I tried on the shoes it was the same thing, too small. I could only get my foot in halfway. Talk about Cinderella's stepsister! Everything was brand new, with tags still attached. My heart was shattered, but I didn't cry, because whenever I cried at home, I was told to turn off the "crocodile" tears.

I looked at my mom and saw that she looked as sad as I felt.

"She must have thought you were a lot smaller than you are. She should have written and asked for your size, but I suppose she wanted it to be a surprise. We'll see what we can do."

That's all she could say at the time. I was a skinny and tall girl for my age. I also had long, thin legs that one of my brothers sweetly called piano legs. That was a great boost to my non-existent sense of self-confidence.

My mother was as good as her word, though, and she did eventually do something about it. She spotted a new girl who had moved in down the street. I didn't know this girl, but she looked as if my lovely new coat would fit her nicely. My mother decided that we would approach this child's mother and offer to sell her, my coat, hat and shoes, brand new fresh from the States.

Mom told me that she would take me downtown and buy me another coat if this one sold.

It sold in fast order and the lady paid in cash. She was delighted with the coat, shoes and hat. I said goodbye to my new clothing and took the money – I forget the amount – home to my mother

When my mother opened her only charge account at Bowring Brothers on Water Street, the first item she purchased on the account was my new coat. It was a grey wool station wagon (to everyone else they were car coats) with a belt and a grey fake fur collar. I loved it! That day I also got a pair of red "Russian" rubber boots that went about four inches above the ankles, and a red shoulder bag to match. I felt like a queen. We wrote my aunt Hann, thanking her for the gifts and telling her how much I liked them. I went out feeling really well-dressed, able to hold my own with the best of them. Station wagon coats were really the "in" thing that year. I began to notice on my way to school that I was seeing a lot of them. But, in my mind, there wasn't one that held a candle to mine.

It was the only one-on-one outing that I ever had with my mother. I had seen her kindness, though, and it had made me feel that she had stopped hating me because of my breech birth that had "almost killed her."

She must have been really ticked off, when the lovely coat lasted only one season. By the next winter I had grown out of it, and it had to be given away to a cousin.

When I was thirteen I started my period. Mom gave me a pile of rags, torn into strips, and I received two pins to keep them in place. She told me that I must wash the rags after use and put them away. This "visitor" would be coming once a month! I was disgusted, and whenever I got the opportunity I tossed the used rags into the stove, claiming that I couldn't find them when they were needed again.

Right about this time my boobs started to grow. Unfortunately for me a slight dark mustache also began to make its appearance on my upper lip. I was horrified. What in the name of God was going on, I wondered. Luckily, unlike my brothers, I had no pimples. It's true that sometimes God is good. So now there was something to take the emphasis away from my rotting front teeth.

If misery does indeed love company, then I was not in too bad a shape. My best friend, Moll, also had a bit of fuzz growing on her upper lip. Then, for the first time, I noticed that my mother was in the same boat. Her teeth were also bad, and she had a few stray hairs where, in my mind, anyway, no woman needed them.

Moll and I discovered a hair remover. It was called Neet, and we pooled our money to buy a tube. We had a big argument about who was going to ask for it at the drugstore. One of us won and we finally got the stuff.

We named our moustaches "Charlie" and removed them whenever we remembered to do so. The hair kept coming back like a bad smell, and we finally read the instructions. Nowhere on the tube was it written that the product was for permanent removal. We were too scared to try anything else, and we consoled ourselves that we still had our lovely long, dark hair. Mine had copper highlights that I loved.

By the start of grade eight, some of my lovely copper highlights began to turn white. Talk about an identity crisis! Going grey at thirteen! It was almost too much for me. I still did have my fine brain, though, and I was turning out some very nice poetry, and doing very well in school and never once did I get the strap for not having my homework done. I did get the strap for going to a forbidden movie, which I was stupid enough to confess to the teacher. Sister Edward, of the washroom scrubbing, visited me again in grade eight. We were lectured on Friday, told which movies were on that odious forbidden list. I took notes, but the names of the movies immediately flew out of my head.

Monday morning Sister Edward stood before the class, neat as a pin and not a trace of a moustache.

"Now girls! Did any of you go the movies on Saturday?" Sister Edward smiled benignly as she asked the question.

I had seen a Jane Powell musical on the weekend, in which the harlot had worn a bathing suit in one scene and a skimpy dance costume in another. She had also kissed a couple of sailors. She had no trace of a moustache, and I thought that she was gorgeous – petite, blonde and absolutely lovely. All of the girls I'd spoken to about the movie thought she was wonderful, too, and we had agreed that she sure could sing! This movie was on the forbidden list.

Nobody said anything in response to the teacher's question, because it's not easy to tell lies in unison, so Sister Edward, pointer in hand, took to walking the aisles and addressing each girl in turn.

The answer was a uniform "No, Sister!"

I was in the third aisle of seats in the classroom, and my mind was going a mile a minute. My heart was racing. I knew the nuns periodically left the motherhouse and went for car rides with relatives or friends. Maybe she had been on an outing that Saturday, maybe she had seen me in the theatre lineup? Which punishment would hurt the most, the one for lying or the one for going to the forbidden movie? The forbidden movie list was, after all, reputed to be from the Pope himself. I figured that truth would be the safest route. Lying, if in fact she had spotted me, would be sure suicide.

A pathetic picture of guilt, I stared resolutely into the inkwell, clenching my hands. When she reached me she asked in a strangely quiet tone – misleading was what it actually was. "Well, missy? Hands on the desk!"

I crumbled and confessed that I had indeed violated the forbidden movie list and defied the Pope and my teacher, and probably, in the process, tainted at least half of the Catholics in St. John's by my bad example.

Flinging her veil over her shoulders, she turned and walked resolutely back to her desk. I was thinking that scrubbing another washroom might be an enjoyable break just about then, but she yanked open the desk drawer and pulled out her massively thick leather strap.

Then she called me to the front of the room and strode purposefully toward me, brandishing her piece of leather. The rest of the girls waited in silence as my trembling legs carried me forward. There was not a sound or a squirm in the room. Not one of the girls would have been stupid enough to make a move.

"Palms up!"

On the third attempt at keeping my hands out, the palms finally stayed in place. Sister was becoming agitated.

She raised her hand again and brought the strap down with all her weight behind it, first on one of my hands and then the other. I felt close to passing out, but I managed to stagger back to my desk. I could barely see because of the blinding tears. I had promised myself that I wouldn't cry, but promises are made to be broken, and that was a mighty thick leather strap, as hard as Sister Edward herself. My fingers felt as if they had been amputated, and there was a tiny ooze of blood where the skin had been broken on the palm of one hand.

When I finally came back to the land of the living, I took a furtive look at my poor tortured hands. There were huge, mottled welts, which went a good three inches up each wrist.

I sat there and enjoyed the feeling of hatred I felt for Sister Edward. My stepfather's oaths had almost faded from my mind, so I contented myself with simply hating her. Hating her didn't do me any good, but at least the emotion gave me freedom in my mind. She had no way of knowing what I was thinking, unless she happened to notice the evil eye I was giving her.

She didn't even glance my way. Her breathing seemed to be a little ragged, judging by the slight heaving of her chest. I hoped that she would have a heart attack. I figured she deserved it, abusing her authority that way. Of course there was no such thing as child abuse in those days. To this day I still dislike her, but I may be able to forgive her when I grow too old to remember her face.

The strapping didn't do much to shape my character. I went to another forbidden movie the next Saturday. When she asked the usual question on Monday morning I answered a prudent "No, Sister!" So did every other girl in the room.

My mother never did learn I had been strapped that Monday morning. I went home for lunch and kept my mouth shut. To complain would have led to an interrogation, and there was the strong probability of a clout across the head with a wet dishcloth. The nun's and priest's actions were sacrosanct in those days. If a child received a strapping from a holy sister, then that child must have been guilty of breaking some rule in the first place. The teacher was always right, and Catholic parents stood united with them.

I had read somewhere, "It is better to remain silent and be thought a fool, than to speak and remove all doubt." I took that saying to heart and, with my hands behind my back, I told Mom that the day was going just fine, thank you very much.

That same year I won first place in a poetry competition and my picture was in the *Daily News.* I came home from school for lunch, and the paper's photographer was waiting for me in the front room. No smile on my face, of course. I wasn't putting those teeth on display for any reason. Sister Edward did not speak of the poem or the picture. None of the sisters mentioned it. I felt more than a little wounded.

Right about the same time, Mom and I began to have some serious conflicts. She was usually sitting in her rocking chair, often feeling unwell. I grew up seeing my brothers kiss her cheek before they left the house. I began to do the same thing at lunchtime, and invariably she would look up at me and spit out, "Judas!"

Everyone knew what Judas had done, that he was history's ultimate traitor. I was never able to figure out what he had to do with me or why, in Mom's mind, I deserved that name.

I know that I talked back, and she said that I always had to have the last word. One morning I was leaving for school at the tail end of an argument, and she chased me out the hall. I stupidly ran to the wall instead of through the front door, and she caught me by my hair and banged my head into the wall again and again. Luckily for me the walls in the old house had a lot of give in them, and so I survived without obvious brain damage. By the time I'd recovered from a whopper of a headache, it was time to go home from school for lunch.

At lunchtime I didn't mention our early-morning argument and neither did my mother. We just carried on as if nothing had happened – until the next time, of course.

After each upset I went to confession, consumed with guilt, and was forgiven. Every time I passed a cemetery I scanned the headstones. Sister Edward had told us that any ungrateful child who had the audacity to talk back to a parent would wind up, when dead and buried, with one arm raised above the ground, for all of eternity.

I saw nary an arm sticking up, thank God. There was still some hope for my salvation.

Chapter 20

By the time I reached grade eight another of the fortune teller's prediction came true. After Dad's death my mother had her fortune told by a woman who was reputed to be the best fortune teller in St. John's. She had accurately predicted that my mother would marry a man who worked around buses and cars and who bent his elbow quite a bit. My stepfather was a mechanic, and his elbow was definitely flexible.

Another of her predictions was that my mother would receive money, on a regular basis, from men in uniform. This bit of news, I remember, caused a great deal of hilarity among my mother and her three girlfriends, who boarded with us, after my father's death. The ultimate conclusion among the girls was that Mom would start going out with the Yanks.

The first of my brothers to leave home was Jerry, her "Rock," and his going left a void in her life that nobody could ever hope to fill. He joined the army, winding up in Germany as a member of the Royal Canadian Dragoons, a tank corps.

He sent Mom a portion of his cheque every month.

The next to leave home was Lew, the singer, who became a member of the Princess Patricia's Canadian Light Infantry. His going also left a great void in my mother's life.

True to form, he allotted Mom a portion of his pay on a monthly basis.

Jack was underage, but he forged his birth certificate

and left home one morning, telling Mom that he was joining the army, too. I remember her screaming at him as he went out the hall toward the front door, "Don't you dare! You be home here tonight!"

That evening, after a terribly worrisome day, we received a telegram from him. He was at Camp Petawawa, in Ontario. He probably would have called, but we didn't have a phone.

He also sent Mom part of his pay every month.

My brother Jerry wrote to Mom and me regularly from Germany.

Lew, I remember, also wrote to Mom faithfully. Then he was sent to Korea, and a new round of worrying began as his outfit went right into the fighting zone. They were often mentioned in the newspapers as being under heavy enemy fire. The news sent fear into the hearts of those left at home.

Jack turned up in Korea, and Lew thought he was seeing a ghost. He knew that Jack was underage and that Mom would be crazy with worry, so he went to the commander of their outfit and told him that Jack was underage and should not be left in the thick of the action. As a result, Jack was sent back to Japan, and his life was saved for a while. Mom had a little less to worry about, but the loves of her life were gone from home and all she had left was a snit of a daughter; her youngest son, Bob; and of course, my stepfather, who was, at least, in his sane, sober senses.

I think I might have been tempted to join the military myself if he had still been in his raging cups.

So the cheques continued to roll in. Even Bob and I were contributing in a small way. Since Newfoundland had become the tenth province of Canada, the baby bonus came in every month. It was little enough compared to the money my brothers were sending, but it was our feeble best, and something is always better than nothing when it comes to money.

When Jerry returned from Germany after his tour of duty, my mother took out a fat, brown purse and opened it in front of him. She had saved every penny of the money he sent every month, and she handed Jerry the thick, rolled wads of bills. He was amazed and touched. He went out and bought an almost new used car that very day. I was proud of her and surprised. I hadn't had a clue about her savings.

The most painful episode of my young life was, of course, the loss of my father. Running a close second was something that happened while my three oldest brothers were away in the forces. I know Mother worried about them constantly, but I was not prepared for the hurt I felt, the wound her tongue made in my heart one day.

I was fairly used to being called "Judas" when I kissed her goodbye, but she really blindsided me one day when I bent to kiss her before leaving for school.

She stared straight in my face; her lovely blue eyes were ice-cold, and she looked as if she hated me.

"Don't bother!" she said, turning her face aside. "The three who matter are gone."

I felt the pain like a knife. I knew I wasn't the best daughter in the world, but I was also certain that I was far from being the worst one. That day I reached the point where I just got tired of fighting for a bit of affection.

I didn't say a word. For once I was speechless. There was no reply that would have made a difference, nor would an answer have done anything but lead to an argument. I had no heart left for that.

Me at age 7 – missing my front teeth, but with clean knees. Three months before Dad's death.

LEFT: The end of the good times. Three months before the death of my father. Back row: my eldest brother Jerry, Dad, Lew and my mother. Front row: My brother Jack, my brother Bob and myself. RIGHT: My brother Lew on Allan Square, with his dog Snapper. Note the drain gutters and the unpaved street. Livingstone Street is to the north.

From left to right: My brothers Jerry, Lew and Jack. Bob was too small for this picture, and I don't have a clue where I was at the time. God love 'em all, the long, the short and the tall!

LEFT: Kids of the neighbourhood. Back row on step: me in black coat and hat, others unknown. Front row: Jack perched on step, others unknown. Sorry, kids! RIGHT: Jack, age 4, and me, age 3. Although it looks as if my hand is resting on Jack's knee, it's actually his hand on his knee. The stool we're sitting on is the infamous one I was hefting when I fell over the front steps and broke my collarbone.

My father and mother, Lewis Murphy and Dorothy Kelly, with their first child, baby Jerry. He became known as Mom's "Rock."

The Kirk on Long's Hill, St. Andrew's Presbyterian Church. Catholic children were forbidden to enter any churches other than Catholic ones. Every Good Friday the Kirk put on movies of the Passion and piled on the food and drink. They always got a full house. Lots of hungry Catholics, including me, lined up for a free movie and free food. Surely there could be no sin in that? My stomach decided no.

Water Street as it looked when I did my mother's Christmas shopping at Bowring Brothers. It's dark and quiet, but sentinels of lighted windows wait for the onslaught of morning shoppers.

The bandstand in one of my happiest childhood places, beautiful Bannerman Park. During the war years, marching bands and parades were a regular part of life in St. John's. The music was stirring, the atmosphere vibrant and the soul effortlessly filled to overflowing with thoughts of victory, power and hope. Thanks to the Bannerman Park bandstand, men in uniform can still bring me to a swoon.

Massed troops in formation at one of the parade grounds.

Opening of the National War Memorial on Duckworth Street in St. John's, 1924. Note the hardy folks on the roof: great seats available for those with nerves of steel!

Grade nine class at Presentation High School on Barnes Road. Some of the fancy printing on the board is mine, and the rest is Patricia Field's work.

Convent girl, with attitude, home for lunch. Photo taken in the backyard.

LEFT: Somebody must have told a good joke! Me with my mother's Tickle Cove cushion and the flowers Lew sent her for Easter or Mother's Day. I think he was away in the military at the time, or living in Toronto. RIGHT: Mom and I posing before Lew's flowers. We both look pretty happy.

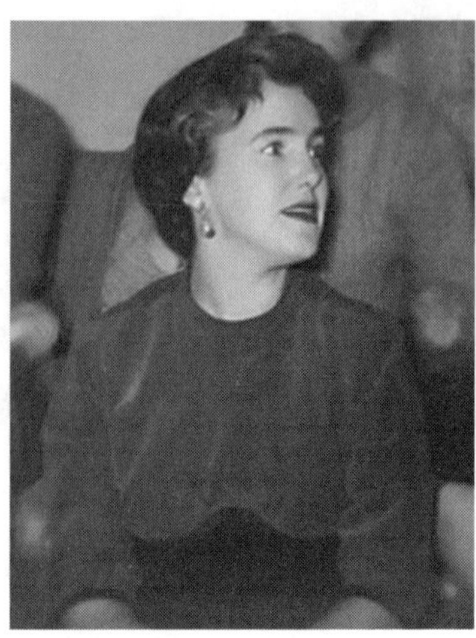

LEFT: Studio shot taken of me in 1958. RIGHT: At a wedding shower thrown for me by some co-workers.

Lew and Shirley – after the days of the Chinese burn.

The new homes on Queen's Road at the south side of Allan Square add a smart, trendy look to the old neighbourhood. Did I really throw stink bombs into those doors?

The house on Allan Square, rebuilt from the bottom up and with new owners. There is no trace of the house in which I grew up, only the memories remain.

Chapter 21

By the time I was thirteen, I was taller than my mother. I was five foot seven – taller than most of the girls in my class.

My mother was just a little over five feet, but then dynamite also comes in small packages.

She had some rather peculiar advice for me about men and sex. She said – distasteful as the comment seems now – that a woman was a mere waste receptacle for men. She also advised me that a man would "put *it* anywhere at all, even a keyhole, if there was any way it could possibly fit."

My two older brothers weren't much more encouraging.

"You play with the bull, you get the horns!"

"If they're old enough to bleed, they're old enough to butcher!"

When talking about a particular girl: "Does she come across?"

I began to give the nunnery serious consideration and wondered if maybe I had the "calling" for a vocation.

Anything would be better than being a waste receptacle for a man was the way I figured it.

Fortunately, my kissing days with the ushers were safely behind me. At least I'd had that much. My rotting teeth kept me from further experimentation; the fuzz of my moustache was the icing on the cake. I determined that my person, the temple of God, as the nuns liked to say, would remain inviolate. My brothers and my mother nicely tied up any loose ends that remained of my curiosity.

I turned to God; where else was there to go? I began to

attend morning Mass on a daily basis. Thankfully my bed was always dry, since I never peed in my new folding cot. The first thing I did when I got up in the morning was to light the fire in the Ideal range. Later on we got an oil stove, and I was relieved of that job. For starting the fire in the coal stove I used paper as a base and then splits and coal. In no time at all, the kettle was boiling and ready for making tea. I always made Cream of Wheat cereal for my mother before I left for school because she was feeling poorly most all of the time. The Cream of Wheat was the bane of my morning existence. My mother could not bear to even look at it if there were any lumps. Try as I might to remove the lumps as they began to appear out of nowhere, there were always a few remaining in the bowl. All hell would break loose, and I was informed that my children, if I was ever stupid enough to have any, would probably starve to death or be unable to walk due to rickets or some other childhood disease.

Any fool knew how to make cereal, she said. "Just boil the water, pour in the cereal and stir."

It could not be any simpler; she was, after all, not demanding eggs Benedict. No matter, I just couldn't manage it without the lumps, rocky ones, and hard as hell. Distinctly unpalatable, especially for someone who had a delicate stomach, as my mother did.

The toast and tea were hard to screw up, and so my mother did have a little sustenance before I left the house for the sanctuary of the big cathedral on the hill.

I was filled with fervour at Mass, castigating myself, time after time, for giving my poor mother a hard time and for not being the daughter she so richly deserved after the hard life she had led.

When I went home for lunch, things were sometimes fine. I discovered my sense of humour and saw that Mom was literally helpless before it. No matter how hard she tried not to laugh, eventually she usually broke up at my antics.

It actually started right after a summer holiday to visit my aunt and my cousins in St. Mary's Bay. While I was there, one of my cousins, Nancy, was sent out to the well with instructions to bring in the jelly, which was setting there.

The next thing we knew, Nancy, who had a sharp sense of humour herself, came charging through the door, without the jelly! She was dead serious this time, though, and her face reflected the gravity of whatever doom had befallen the jelly.

"Blessed Virgin Mary, Mudder of God! Mudder! The whole side is gone out of the jelly!"

It struck my funny bone, and when I went back home, I acted it out for Mom. She thought it was hilarious, and whenever we had company, I was encouraged to "do" Nancy for them.

I did get a little mileage out of my performance, until she tired of it.

It has taken me years to figure out that my mother actually enjoyed fighting. After my stepfather sobered up, I was her combatant of choice.

Whenever my mother and I were having one of our spats, one or the other of my brothers usually walked into the middle of it. Their reactions varied a great deal.

My brother Jack always sang the same song, before he pulled out his harmonica and played it:

"Slap her down agin, Ma!
Make her tell us where she's been.
We don't want our neighbours,
Talkin' 'bout our kin!"

That was a great icebreaker. Even I had to laugh at Jack. He dressed just like Fonzie in *Happy Days*, long before the show went on the air. Stovepipe jeans, black leather jacket and dark hair slicked back in a duck's tail. He was the only one in the family whose teeth were beautiful, white and unblemished.

Jack was too shy to act like the Fonz, but he had a buddy, Eddy, who dressed the same way and had the attitude to go with it. He could have had any girl in town, and he was well aware of his fatal attraction. He did have two distinct flaws as far as I was concerned: he was short and his legs were bowed. The girls didn't seem to mind, though; they literally fell at his feet.

We were going to have a dance, an unheard-of thing! A combined dance – the Mercy girls would be there, too, and we were all allowed, even encouraged, to have dates for the event.

My God! It was a shock to our systems. Of course the dance was to be chaperoned by the combined sisters of the Mercy and Presentation convents. It was to be held in the auditorium of St. Patrick's Hall, which was a Catholic boys' school.

Where in the name of God was I supposed to get a date? I racked my brain, but that didn't get results. Finally my brother Jack got wind of my problem and enlisted the aid of the darkly handsome and very short Eddy, who, for reasons known only to a Higher Power and his own healthy libido, promptly agreed to be my escort. His mouth was probably watering at the thought of all the female flesh that would be available at this dance.

The next problem was an outfit for me. I had only my uniform and a few skirts, sweaters and slacks. They wouldn't do for my very first dance.

About six months before this event, my father's sister-in-law and her daughter, whose name was the same as mine, died tragically in a car accident in New York. The US relatives had sent some clothing, and, inexplicably, a pair of living room drapes to Mom. There were a few dresses there that fit my mother and which were quite pretty. There was also a hot pink satin dress with a full skirt, long sleeves and scooped-out neckline.

As soon as I looked at the neckline, I knew my boobs would never stretch to the occasion. My friend Moll suggested that maybe we could augment them with toilet tissue or socks. We decided on the socks, because toilet tissue was in short supply in our house. We had the *Evening Telegram* on standby for the washroom, but that simply would not do for the bosom of the dress.

Moll and I decided that we would both remove our moustache fuzz with the ever-faithful Neet. It would not do for me to go to my first dance with hair on my upper lip. The teeth I wasn't too worried about. Jack's friend Eddy had seen them many times. Besides, I really had no intention of smiling that night, in front of all those Mercy girls! No way.

I put my hair in rags the night before the big occasion. The rags stayed in too long, and my hair, normally manageable, stood every which way in pure frizz.

As to the shoes, I think I wore my black penny loafers, a bit rundown at the heels and definitely past their prime. That's what I used for school, and they were the only ones I had. I already knew they wouldn't go well with the hot pink dress, but "when in Rome do as the Romans" did not always apply in my life. I knew that I would never be able to compete with the moneyed girls from Mercy Convent. I did, however, take the pennies out of my shoes.

I don't know where my brothers were, but if they had been around I'm sure they would have scraped together a few bucks to get me a decent pair of shoes.

I don't remember Eddy calling for me; I have no memory of how we got to the dance.

I do remember, however, my horror when I learned that the girls and their escorts were expected to take part in the "grand march." I nearly died as I walked beside Eddy – I was able to see the top of his sleek black hair. I practically twisted myself in half an attempt to make myself appear shorter.

Then I suddenly remembered Captain O'Grady, a veteran soldier who came to the school once a week to give us an hour-long physical education lesson. He was a fine-looking man who carried a baton and wore a khaki shirt and khaki breeks, a brown tie and brown leather boots that reached to the knees. He cut a dashing figure, and his demeanour appealed to me greatly.

Our physical education class consisted of marching and learning proper deportment. We were to wind up looking like a good bunch of soldiers if Captain O'Grady did his job correctly, and he definitely did his best.

During the lessons he stood in the centre of the room holding his baton and put us into formation, two girls in each line. We had no marching music. Our instructor always said "Hup, two, three, four!" and we would begin our straggle around the hall.

He periodically barked, in the best military manner, "Shoulders back! Stomach in! Chest out! Head up! Hup, two, three, four!"

I desperately tried to push out my practically non-existent chest at his commands. I did manage to stand tall, tummy tucked in and shoulders back.

Just when I needed him, standing in that bloody lineup outside the hall, the image of Captain O'Grady flooded back into my memory. I forgot about short Eddy and reached to my impressive full height, tucked in the tummy, pushed back the shoulders, pushed out what there was of the boobs and began the walk into the room, feeling, for a brief period, like an Amazon.

Eddy promptly shrank to his proper height, and I was able to get a better look at the top of his lovely head of black hair. There it was! The beginnings of a bald spot on the crown of his head. There was no doubt about it, he was cute, but I figured he would be getting bald at an early age. His problem. I had my own problems.

By this time we were inside the hall. Eddy's hungry eyes were darting to every cute female in the room. My sense of humour surfaced right about then, and I almost stopped walking as I imagined myself back at Allan Square, in the safety and relative comfort of my folding cot. But I resolutely walked forward in the best tradition of Captain O'Grady.

I have never been able to figure out why I forced myself to go to that dance. Eddy deposited me at a table, where I scooted as close to the wall as I could. He plunked a pop in front of me (nice of him). Then he promptly caved in to his libido and disappeared for the remainder of the evening. I noticed him twirling some beauty or another around the floor all night, the prick! I never moved from my seat.

I don't know how I got home. I certainly don't remember Eddy escorting me, but get there I did. I stood inside the front door and laughed until I cried.

The next morning I regaled my mother with stories of the good time that was had by *almost* all. Then I went back to my cot, pleading a very bad headache, which I milked for the rest of the day. Amazing what trauma can do to the young female body. God love you, Eddy – I hope you are as bald as an eagle, wherever you are!

Chapter 22

My mother's health began to seriously deteriorate the year I was in grade ten. She began to faint regularly and had to have smelling salts on hand at all times. Many days she was too ill to get out of bed, complaining of chest pains, constant nausea and a feeling of having a tight band around her head. The "tight band" feeling was probably an indication of high blood pressure, but I didn't know that then. The years of worrying about her absent boys, who were scattered around the world, one of them in active combat in Korea, were beginning to take their toll on her already delicate health.

The nuns at school knew of her illness and allowed me to come in late, so that I could do for her before I went to school. Many times I was off for a full week at a time, and I began to feel that I was the mistress of the kitchen. Cooking, cleaning and anything else needed doing were my jobs. She seemed to appreciate my help.

Then she'd suddenly make what appeared to be a remarkable recovery, reminding me of Lazarus rising from the dead at Jesus' command, frightening his relatives half to death in the process. I always felt I'd been doing a half-decent job of keeping things in order, but after she was on her feet and relatively mobile, nothing that I had done suited her, nothing at all.

She finally went to a doctor in the neighbourhood. He diagnosed hysterics. He must have been crazy. There was nothing hysterical about my mother's illness. He must have mentioned shock treatment, because I heard her pleading with my stepfather that, no matter what happened, he would never sign any papers allowing it. He promised, and he kept that promise.

My stepfather must have had a core of mercy running somewhere through his alcohol-soaked veins. One day, without warning, a pickup truck pulled up to the front door, and a wringer washer was unloaded. It was put in the lobby close to the cold-water tap. It made one godawful racket. I don't know how we managed the laundry before the washer came. Maybe I've suppressed the memory. There was, of course, no such thing as a dryer, and in the winter, the laundry, in all its grey, damp glory was strung on lines in the kitchen – ideal extra dampness for a woman in my mother's precarious state of health.

As soon as the weather began to warm up, the laundry was hung on lines that criss-crossed the backyard. I remember reams and reams of grey work socks I had laundered swinging madly in the wind. Any dirt that the cold water could not remove remained in the socks, leaving them, when dry, hard as rocks. I didn't care, because I had not reached the stage of wearing them, so there was no point of worrying about the aesthetics of laundry. The socks had been banged around inside the washer; therefore, they were clean, if a bit stiff. What did they want from me, anyway?

Somewhere between my thirteenth and fifteenth birthdays, a letter arrived from my father's sister in the States, my aunt Hann. Unlike the other letters, this one was addressed to my mother, not to me.

My mother did not mention what was in the letter right away, but I overheard her talking to a few of her lady friends who had dropped in for a visit.

"Can you just imagine it? She had the bloody nerve to ask me to send my only daughter to them in the US? New York, yet! The Bronx! I hear that's no better than Allan Square. All these years, when they didn't care if we lived or died. Although I must admit his sister did remember the girl and sent her a few dollars every now and then. I've no time for them at all, and I never did!

"Why, if it wasn't for my own sister and her husband, after the youngsters' father died, there was many a time we would have starved. We had nothing. My sister and her husband shared everything they had with us, and God knows they weren't floating with money, God love them. His relatives in the States can fly to hell's fiery flames, as far as I'm concerned!"

"Sure that's true enough for you!" came the scandalized reply from one of the ladies.

"Oh, my God! What a bloody gall them people in the States have got! Just imagine it! Just when she's getting big enough to be a bit of a help to you. God knows ye've had a hard time of it, my love, so you have!" from the other one.

The first lady cut in. "God knows that's true. Although I suppose it did get a bit easier after the second fella sobered up. At least then ye didn't have to worry about where yer next slice of baloney was coming from, did ye?"

My mother, however, had tired of the topic and quickly changed the subject. She would let people go only so far. These two friends were fast approaching the bar of her privacy. They got no more information from her that day and they soon got bored, said their goodbyes, and left.

I went into the kitchen, rubbing my eyes as if I had been napping.

"Bloody newsmongers!" my mother was muttering, obviously regretting her confidences.

She then told me what Aunt Hann's letter was all about. My aunt had offered to take me, body and bones, into the Promised Land, to be with all of Dad's relatives. His mother and father were both still alive at that time. Strangely enough, I had absolutely no desire to go, no urge to leave Allan Square. Maybe it was the Stockholm Syndrome. My mother tried to gauge my reaction. I gave none, just listened to her.

"You know what they want, don't you?" she stared at me keenly. "They want a maid, that's what they want. It certainly can't be love; they don't even know you or your brothers. They're looking for someone to take care of those two old people. Your father's mother was a cold bitch when I first met her. I can't imagine that time has done anything to improve her. You'd be nothing but a bloody slave there. Stuck in some apartment in the Bronx! Not bloody likely! Imagine, they're talking about sending the prepaid ticket! I've already written her and told her she can stick her ticket where the monkey stuck his peanuts. You're not going, and that's the end of it!"

My mother was furious. I was used to seeing her furious, but her anger was usually directed at me. This passion was because she didn't want to lose me. I consoled myself that she must love me after all. If she didn't love me, I reasoned, she would have gladly accepted the ticket and waved a relieved goodbye to her "house devil and street angel."

Later, when Moll and I were sitting on my front steps, I told her about my aunt's offer.

She said, "Would you want to go, if she let you? My mom says that in New York they shoot people in the streets for no reason at all."

I thought hard about my brothers and my mother, and I answered in the negative, but deep inside, my sense of self-worth had definitely gone up a notch or two. My father's people wanted me! I found it hard to understand. Why would anyone want me?

Then, as the moon began to dip its light over Allan Square, Moll and I broke into our rendition of "Cruising Down the River."

We finally said goodnight and went to our homes and beds. I dreamed of getting shot dead on the wild streets of New York.

In the dream, all my father's relatives were watching and they pretended not to know me from Adam. When I woke up I was glad to find myself at home, relatively safe and sound.

The American relatives never broached the subject to my mother again. That must have been some letter she sent them!

Chapter 23

When "the three who mattered" came back from their tours of duty in the military, they always went from the kitchen through my mom and stepfather's bedroom, then through mine, and from there into the front room where they slept together in a huge bed.

My stepfather slept on the side of the bed next to my room, which still had a curtain instead of a door. The statue of the "Little Flower" was on a shelf next to my stepfather, and his loose change was at her feet.

Whenever I passed through to go to my bed, he opened his eyes swiftly and checked his change. I felt like picking it up and tossing it in his face, which would have served him right. You wouldn't know but he was in a homeless shelter, and all his possessions in danger of being whipped away from right under his nose, you might say.

When they returned home, the three boys quickly fell back into a routine of kissing our mother good night. They were not too quiet about it, either. Even now, I can still hear my stepfather, grumbling and groaning about having to get up in the morning for work. What did they think he was anyway, a fucking workhorse?

Mom woke screaming every night when my brother Jerry, the one who looked so much like Dad, kissed her lightly on the cheek. She thought he *was* Dad and bolted up, terrified, screaming out my father's name. That did not go over too well with her second husband, who also woke up screaming, but not from nightmares. After a number of ghostly episodes like that, the boys stopped kissing her on the cheek, and each of them lightly kissed her on the part of the blanket, under which they presumed her feet were resting. Eureka! The end of the nightmares and the screaming. I could finally get some rest after they passed through my room. They usually fought and pushed each other for territory in their bed, before we all finally fell into a deep, exhausted sleep.

Jerry and Lew regularly got into battles over which one of them had been in the best outfit in their army days. I became so sick of hearing about the heroics of the Royal Canadian Regiment in active combat in Korea versus that of the Royal Canadian Dragoons, resting on its laurels in Germany. It got so bad that I was ready to throw up at the very thought of khaki uniforms. Things got so heated at times that my mother, tiny as she was, had to insert herself between them so they wouldn't kill each other. I kept out of the way of clenched fists as often as I could. Personally, I was fully prepared to let them get on with it. I have to confess there were many times when I cheerfully wished them back in their barracks. The flat was just too small for all of us, but my mother was happy to have them back home, relatively safe and sound.

Even when the three who mattered came back, I still did not kiss my mother goodbye. I didn't really hold it against her that she hadn't wanted me to kiss her, but I have learned through life that my pain runs deep and has great staying power.

And so we carried on in that fashion. I never kissed my stepfather in my life, nor did I ever feel any affection for him, not the slightest.

My eldest brother, Jerry, had always written me faithfully from Germany. I felt cherished by him. One day I received a letter from a girl in England. Jerry had met her while on a weekend there, and he had given her my address. We corresponded for quite a while and I enjoyed it, but the memory of her brief fling with my brother died a quiet death, and soon I didn't hear from her anymore.

Jerry and Lew began going to the Catholic Youth Club on Harvey Road. There was no drinking allowed, and half the Catholic married couples in St. John's had met there.

The first night he went there, Jerry met the girl who was destined to become his wife. When she met me she noticed my rotting teeth with the vampire fangs hanging down over them. She mentioned to him that I could be quite pretty if my teeth were fixed. The next thing I knew, I was at a dentist's office on Church Hill. He took one look and I guess figured he'd never get paid if he tried to fix them. So he told me to come back on a certain day. He was going to yank out the whole works. They weren't much, but they were all I had. I was terrified.

I dutifully turned up at his office on the appointed day; my heart was thumping out of my body. I recited poetry while I waited for his grand entrance: "I wandered lonely as a cloud." Then I was out like a light, and it took me five hours to wake up. (Even without gas I had always been a heavy sleeper.) I was totally gummy! It was the most horrible feeling I had ever known. I have no idea how I got home.

In the process of my "healing," the roof of my mouth collapsed, adding to my misery. It managed somehow to heal itself in about a month without benefit of any medicine. As soon as it was feasible, I went to a bootleg denturist who worked on Livingstone Street, and I acquired top and bottom dentures. I had to admit that I looked better.

A couple of years later, Moll, whose top teeth had also been spoiling her looks, promptly had hers removed, and she also got some new teeth. I think she was able to save her bottom ones, but I couldn't swear to that.

My hair, which had first showed strands of white in grade eight, was progressing slowly toward its destined colour; I still had mostly dark hair and blue eyes. I didn't look half bad.

I also had my wisps of dark hair on my upper lip, but there was always the ever faithful tube of Neet. It did the job for me and for Moll. We promised each other, between fits of the giggles, that whoever of us kicked off last would make sure the other's moustache would be next to invisible in the casket.

I took to looking in the mirror again, able to do so now without shedding a tear. I looked okay, but faced the fact that I would never send a man's heart racing with anything remotely resembling passion.

Time was to prove me wrong.

Chapter 24

The summer holidays of my school years were fraught with worry. We didn't find out until returning for the first day of school in September whether or not we had passed. The Mother Superior went around to each of the classrooms and read out the marks, giving the verdict at the end of her reading. We could almost hear the sighs of relief at the end of each session. Some girls with lower marks were sent to what the girls referred to as the "dumb" class – or the B one. Anyone in the B class did not have the opportunity to take Latin, chemistry and other subjects that required an extra bit of brainpower or effort.

I was in the B class for two years, grades four and five, which happened to be the years my stepfather's alcoholic rantings were at their height. Personally, I wouldn't have known that there were two classes for every grade, except that the girls from the A classes looked very alert and more awake than I felt.

Mother Bridget, an elderly nun who had a fearsome reputation, presided over grade five B. If there was any extra grey matter clinging to any brain in the room, Mother Bridget was one nun who knew how to find it and root it out into the light of day. You couldn't hide one damn thing from her. I was not afraid of this sister. I absolutely loved her! She let some of her "pets" dust the desks after school, and she always handed out a few chocolates in return for the labour. She may have reached me through my stomach and my weakness for sweets, but she sure reached me. I still cherish her memory.

In spite of the worry of passing or failing the school year, the long, lovely summers called me. My mother always let me sleep in late. When I finally crawled out of my folding cot, everyone else but Mom had gone their various ways for the day. I sat at the table, listened to Irish music on the radio and had a cup of tea with some toast.

The next step was into the lobby for a wash in cold water. If I was not fully awake, that cold-water wash usually did it. I used Sunlight; a heavy-duty soap guaranteed to clear away all the dirt. My friends wondered how my legs became so shiny. It was the scrubbing with Sunlight that did it. They glistened. After my wash I prepared a sandwich of bread and butter and filled a pop bottle with water and powdered lemon crystals. Sugar was added. The top was then plugged with rolled-up paper and the bottle was shaken until it was ready to explode. If it didn't leak it was safe to take on an outing. Soon I was ready to head for my favourite summer playground, Bannerman Park. It was enclosed by wrought iron fences in my time; that was one of the things I liked about it. I have no idea why I always went there alone so often during the week. Helen, Moll and I had a pact that we'd go there every Saturday and spend the whole day. When I went alone I liked to write poetry, so I generally took a few scraps of paper and a pencil with me. I actually quite enjoyed being alone.

I took the Rennie's Mill Road entrance to the park because I liked the grand houses, the wealthy atmosphere of the street, and the fact that Mom had worked as a serving girl in one of them.

I always ran for a huge tree that was just inside the gate of the park and threw myself on the ground under it. There I stayed for a while, staring up at its full height and watching the leaves tossing about. It made me feel so peaceful that I sometimes stared for half an hour or more, all alone and happy as a lark.

Then I headed farther into the park, always stopping at the water fountain and half drowning myself, before I went into the playground. I tried all the equipment, ending with the swings, where I swung until I was beat out and in danger of flinging myself over the top bar. Finally I disembarked and began wandering toward the lower end of the park. There were no nasty perverts in the park in those halcyon days, so it was safe to wander through anywhere at all. (Either there were no perverts or else my guardian angels were working overtime; anyway, I never did see anyone who looked the least bit threatening.)

In the east end of the park, I sat on a bench and devoured my lunch. The lemon-crystal drink was always wonderful, usually swallowed in one gulp.

After a short rest I wandered over to the Rennie's Mill Road side of the park. There I walked around slowly, head down, eyes scanning the ground, which was like another world, because there were scads of white rubbery things scattered all over it. One of my friends, on one of the rare times when I had company in the park, had told me the things were called "French safes." Why French I had no idea, but she also told me they had been discarded the night before by the Yanks, who took their girlfriends to the park, where they lay down on the grass and did *"it."* By using those things, my friend told me, the girls could not get pregnant, and neither the man nor the girl would get a disease.

"But why don't they pick them up later?" I asked her.

"Are you nuts?" she retorted, "Pick up those filthy things? They're not idiots you know, just horny."

With that she stepped on one of them, and white gunk squirted all over her shiny black shoes. We laughed our heads off as she cleaned it off with grass. I wondered if I would have to tell about the episode in confession, and I promptly decided that, in any case, there was no way I was confessing it. The definition of mortal sin, according to what I had learned in religion class, was "Mortal sin is sin whose object is grave matter and which is also commited with full knowledge and deliberate consent." Except for the "full knowledge" part, the matter, I decided, was not confession material. So my conscience was clear.

One day during the summer, I hit the jackpot during a

visit to the park. In the Yanks' playground I spied, among white ground cover, a wallet! I glanced around to see if anyone was near, gingerly picked it up and slipped it into my pocket. When I reached the exit I normally used, the Military Road one, I sat on a bench and examined the wallet. As I remember it, there was no identification, but there was money! I don't remember the exact amount, but it looked like a fortune to me. There must have been at least ten folded bills and some change.

I left the park and slowly made my way home. It was now about three in the afternoon. If I kept the money and threw away the wallet, I reasoned to myself, that would certainly be a matter for confession. The priest would probably demand that the money be handed over to the church for charity purposes. I figured they'd never find anybody in more need of charity than I was, so turning it over to the church coffers wasn't an option. If I gave it to my honest mother, she would do her best to find the owner and I wouldn't get one red cent. That didn't seem fair to me.

So I squeezed out five dollars in ones and put them in my shoe. When I was safely standing on a little of the money, I felt a lot better. I went home and gave my mother the wallet. Later on I heard an ad on VOCM radio.

"Found in Bannerman Park, a wallet containing money. No identification in the wallet. Upon advising of the amount of money in the wallet, the owner may pick up his property." Our address was given.

No phone number was given, because we didn't have a phone. I quickly realized that whoever owned the money would never be able to give a correct amount to my mother, and then she would know I had taken some of it. The sole of my shoe was burning and my face began to flush red. Guilt is a terrible thing. I wondered if I could carry it off?

I went out to play and took a walk along Military Road to a candy shop that sold bullseyes. I bought a Graham Sandwich chocolate bar, a bottle of beer (pop) and some bullseyes.

It was way too risky to spend any of my fortune in our

own neighbourhood. Somebody would wonder where in hell's flames the money had come from for the candy. Everybody knew we were poor as church mice. I sat on the steps at the top of Garrison Hill and devoured the whole works.

If the owner of the wallet ever turned up, not another word was ever said about it, not to me, anyway.

That day of the wallet was one of my best days in the park. Normally I was a very honest little girl, but hunger sometimes transforms honesty. I didn't feel guilty at all, although I did recite a heartfelt Act of Contrition that night.

After a tidy little burp, I drifted peacefully off to sleep.

The remainder of the money stayed in my shoe. I disposed of it judicially over the period of a week. After my initial gorging, I remembered my friend Moll and gave her a chocolate bar. She looked at me kind of funny, but didn't ask why I suddenly had disposable cash. No point, after all, of kicking a gift horse in the mouth. I didn't tell her about finding the wallet, because I figured that if nobody knew, nobody could tell.

I still think I handled it the only way I could have done. I didn't say the only way I should have done. I could have given it intact to my mother. But then I would not have had any reward for my honesty. I didn't keep all of it. I could have done so.

It was a mighty fine day in Bannerman Park.

Chapter 25

During the long, lovely days of summer, the kids from Allan Square escaped as often as possible from the hot street. We went swimming at Kent's Pond and Rennie's River.

One of our favourite places to spend a day was Bowring Park. We walked there quite often and spent the entire day going from area to area within the park. We swam in the pool, climbed on the Peter Pan statue and took a small boat out on the little pond, where we were suddenly moving among the swans. They shared their home with us without complaining or getting excited. They were used to people. It was a different world for us. I was always nervous about being out on the pond in a boat. Getting back to shore was always a great relief for me.

Bowring Park was absolutely alive with flowers. There was and still is a lovely old rambling building with a wide veranda. It was called the Bungalow, and they sold snacks, ice cream and pop. Sometimes we'd have a dollar to spend, other days we didn't even have a nickel. We enjoyed the days when we had some cash to spend.

On other days we set out on a fairly long hike up to Signal Hill and visited Cabot Tower, where Marconi received the first transatlantic wireless message. There were all kinds of places to explore up there. We probed inside the wreckage of a building that had once been a military hospital. I was picky and I worried about all the old germs and whether or not they were really dead, or simply lying dormant, waiting to spring back to life. I guess they were dead, because we all survived.

There was a large pond called Deadman's Pond, and we imagined all the poor people who had died there. There was another place where, it was rumoured, people had been hanged. We always blessed ourselves when we passed there. You never know about spirits, they can appear from out of nowhere. We took no chances.

We sat as near to the edge of the cliffs as we could and convinced each other that we could see England across the vast expanse of the Atlantic. Every now and then we were so blinded by the sun on the rippling water that our eyes began to play tricks and we were sure our vision was gone forever. On the verge of panic, we turned to thoughts of home and made our way back to the relative safety of life on Allan Square.

No matter how scared we were, there was always great consolation in the Catholic custom of the sign of the Cross. We blessed ourselves whenever we passed a disabled person and piously murmured "God bless the Mark!" That was meant to prevent any such affliction from ever settling on us.

In later years, I've wondered how the poor person on the other side of the sign of the Cross must have felt. If we passed a person with St. Vitus's dance, which caused them to jump and thrash uncontrollably, we blessed ourselves. If we passed a blind person, we blessed ourselves. If we stepped on a crack, which was bound to break our mothers' backs, we blessed ourselves. We were busy little girls, or at least our arms were busy. When we grew a bit older and wiser and kinder, we didn't do that when we saw people who were different from us.

We made the odd trip down to the harbour and sat quietly watching the big boats coming and going. Every now and then we sang a bit of the song "The Big Ship Sails Through the Illey Alley O." Sometimes we played hide and seek. We called the game "H'ist yer sails and run!" There was no shortage of places to hide on the waterfront. We gagged when we saw the fishermen, standing on the corner of Baird's wharf, with their hands stuck down the gullets of huge codfish. The fish were all sold pretty quickly. A steady stream of customers arrived one day as we watched. The men had other fish lined up on the top of boxes so that the customers could take their pick.

I never ate fish. My mother had gotten a bone caught in her throat sometime in her past, and it had given her such a fright that fish was never again cooked in our house, with the exception of lobster, which was a real treat for everyone but me. I hated the stuff and still do.

* * * * *

Topsail Beach was another great place to go swimming when I was a kid. The scenery was fantastic. You could see Bell Island and another smaller island called Kelly's Island from the beach. One day Moll and I took the bus to the beach, and we spent the whole day there. We had neglected to ensure that we had money for the bus trip home. As a matter of fact, we were flat broke, so we decided there was nothing for us to do but hitchhike.

We went across Topsail Road from the beach and stood by the side of the road, looking, we hoped, suitably dejected. We didn't have any fear in those days of getting picked up by a pervert, although I'm sure there were loads of them around.

Anyway, along comes a car with a lone male occupant. He motioned us into the back seat and asked where we were headed. We told him Allan Square. Then we immediately began acting like two nuts, carrying on like crazy and laughing hysterically. He kept looking back at us in the rear-view mirror with a quizzical expression on his face. He was probably wondering what the hell he had ever done to deserve having the likes of us two visited upon him.

He drove down Waterford Bridge Road, and we didn't think he was going the wrong way, because Allan Square could be reached from there, too.

The next thing we knew, he'd pulled the car into a long driveway, which led to a very large red brick building. He brought the car to a screeching halt and jumped out quickly, opening the back door in a swift motion.

"C'mon girls, get out!" he ordered. "You're home. Enjoy your evening, and the next time you're allowed out, remember to bring your crayons!"

He took off with a fierce squeal of tires. He had dropped us in front of the Waterford Hospital. Everyone in town simply referred to it as the Mental.

We didn't think we had acted crazy enough for such treatment. We decided against trying to hitch another ride; who knew where the next person might drop us off? We used shank's mare to get home. It was quite a long walk, but not as far as it would have been from Topsail Road.

Moll and I were absolutely starving on another of our outings, and we decided to stop at a restaurant on the corner of Bates Hill for a bite to eat. We checked our pockets and found that between the two of us we had about two dollars and twenty cents, enough for an order of chips and a Coke, and we could share a piece of coconut cream pie. We made our decision and hit the steps of the restaurant. A bonus about this particular place was that it was frequented by Yanks. We might get to stare at some cute ones while we ate.

The waitress came along to our table and dropped off two menus. Moll and I, acting as if we had all the money in the world, took our time selecting the food. Against all reason we decided to have a hot turkey sandwich each and a small Coke. We could barely wait for the food to come. Our mouths were actually watering.

There were two small problems, though. Number one, there were no Yanks in the room. The only two customers were an older man and woman at the far end of the restaurant. Number two problem was the state of our finances. The meal would cost more than we had in our pockets. We placed the order anyway.

The waitress came with our food and we dug into it like the two starving critters we were.

When we were done, Moll looked at me and whispered,

"This is going to cost more than we've got. What will we do?"

As if I should know!

The waitress dropped the bill off with a smile and a flourish. She then went to attend another table that had just been filled. We owed the utterly unreachable sum of ten dollars for our hot turkey sandwiches and cokes.

Our backs up against the wall, we sat mulling over the problem.

The poor waitress took the order from the newcomers and went into the kitchen to see to it.

I beckoned Moll and she handed over her two dollars to add to mine. We stood and nonchalantly walked to the front of the restaurant and laid the bill with our four dollars on top, beside the cash register.

We walked to the front door of the restaurant, but we were running inside. We took off up Bates Hill and ran all the way to Allan Square, glancing over our shoulders to make sure nobody was in hot pursuit.

At the bottom of our street, Moll complained that she was feeling sick. She turned as white as a sheet and I watched in horror as she threw up what had been one beautiful sandwich. I didn't feel at all unwell. In fact the whole meal was sitting very nicely in my stomach.

Moll cleaned herself up with a few napkins we had taken from the restaurant and she bemoaned her fate and loss of nutrition.

"That's God!" she moaned and coughed. "It's His punishment for what we done. That poor waitress will have to pay for that order herself. We're some bad, b'y, we are!"

I agreed that what we had done was indeed bad. But I did not think her vomiting was a direct punishment from God. Why would He punish only one of us? My stomach felt just dandy, but I had to admit my conscience was prickling.

By this time Moll was in tears. I was becoming irritated and worried.

"My God, girl! Pull yourself together. There's nothing we can do about it now, anyway. If you go home crying, your mother will find out. I know you'll spill your guts. She'll beat the living shit out of you, and then she'll tell my mother, and my mother will beat the living shit out of me, and then they'll both have our guts for garters. Now tell me, what good will that do us? It will spoil my whole meal. Yours is already ruined anyway. Don't go making it worse."

Moll calmed down, even though she told me she still felt as sick as a dog.

"Never mind!" I burped as I consoled her. "We'll go to confession Saturday and all will be forgiven. The priest can't tell on us. They're not allowed to tell what they hear in confession."

To make her feel even better I said, "It's okay, Moll, really. When we get a bit of money someday we'll light a candle for that waitress. She didn't even get a tip, the poor bitch. We'll go back with the six dollars when we save it up and we'll tell them we found it on the restaurant steps, that some customer must have dropped their change on the way out."

Strangely enough, the very next day I received a letter from my aunt Hann in the States. There was ten dollars in it; she usually only sent two dollars. I figured she must have won really big at bingo.

"An Act of God!" Moll intoned piously as we made our way back to Bates Hill.

Our waitress wasn't there, thank God. She would have recognized us for sure. We went to the cash register and handed over $6, the amount we owed.

The lady who took the cash beamed at us as she said, "My God! It's wonderful to see such honest girls."

We straightened our halos and headed for home.

Moll said, "Now we don't have to tell it in confession, do we? Thank God for that and you still got $4 left."

We went to the corner store and bought some candy to help speed along the rotting of our teeth.

Chapter 26

Medical care was scarce in my childhood. People didn't run back and forth to the doctor for every little ache or pain. There was no such thing as a "yearly checkup" in my time, either. As a matter of fact, I don't even recall seeing a doctor until the time came for me to go out to work.

We did, however, have home-administered health care. As far as our family is concerned, it seems to have done its job. With the exception of my brother Jack, who passed away at thirty, the rest of us have been granted the biblical three-score years and ten. Mom's "Rock" passed away at the age of seventy-one.

Each season of my childhood brought forth its own complaints and suitable remedies. For each malady there was a time-honoured treatment, and my mother seemed to know them all.

For "summer complaint" we were given Extract of Wild Strawberry. It worked like a charm. Be gone stomach flu!

For a tonic she dosed us in the spring and fall with "Brick's Tasteless." It was an over-the-counter concoction that was supposed to clean the blood. I quite enjoyed its taste and opened my mouth like a baby bird to take it. I think there was wine in it. We didn't give any to the stepfather, of course, after he had sobered up. To heck with his health, anyway, I thought to myself. He doesn't need this stuff. He had his raw-egg concoction to build up his constitution. God alone knows what it did to his cholesterol. Of course, there was no such thing as cholesterol at the time. If there had been, his numbers would have flown right off the chart.

Castor oil was also given on a regular basis, followed by the proverbial spoonful of sugar, or, if we had any, a peppermint knob, which is a hard-as-a-rock, pink-and-white-striped candy. Anything that helped the medicine go down, as the song says, was fine by me. Unfortunately, neither the sugar nor the candy did much to stop the relentless decaying of my teeth.

Cod liver oil was sold in a Gerald S. Doyle blue bottle. That was the one I really hated. I didn't care about the decaying teeth; I would have taken any amount of sugar to get that stuff to go down. Mom's anger, if we didn't open up our gobs, was strong enough to overcome any foul taste. Actually, she really didn't need to give us the candy or the sugar. In my case, fear alone would have done it.

Worm medication was given to banish ringworm. I suppose it worked. I never checked.

Skin rashes were a problem, always. At one point in time I developed sores on my hands – and ankles yet! They had started as tiny watery blisters and, after vigorous scratching on my part, quickly developed into oozing sores. I did not tell my mother, and my black school stockings clung to the sores and stuck fast. I had to sleep in them, which didn't help, but it hurt too much to yank them away from the sores. I was a real chicken about pain, and not too careful about hygiene, either.

Of course, the sores just got messier and more painful. I worried myself sick about them. I really had no reason for not telling my mother, but I never did.

Mom finally noticed the sores on my hands and, upon closer inspection, the marks on the stockings. She was very angry because I had not told her about the problem.

The reason I didn't tell anyone was plain and simple fear. I was terrified that I was a victim of leprosy.

Before Mom found out, I haunted the Gosling Memorial Library on Duckworth Street, researching the disease. I found tome after tome, chock full of information and pictures. The pictures I really didn't need, and the information I sucked into my already addled brain only added to my problems.

Treatment was at hand. My mother mercilessly yanked the stockings away from the sores and set about preparing a poultice, which consisted of boiling hot water poured over white bread. I watched in horror as she boiled the kettle. The next thing I knew, a searing hot poultice was pressed onto the sore. There was no way of getting any relief from the scalding. I nearly died from the pain. Then the poultice was wrapped in a bandage made from an old pillowcase. The whole mess was then tied in place with another strip of the same pillowcase.

The identical procedure was followed for the sores on my hands. Oh, the agony of it all! I was about twelve years old at the time. Mom said it was the "Seven Year Itch." I recovered, of course, after the administration of more poultices and some evil-smelling salve. The cure didn't take seven years, not even close, thank God. The sores never came back.

Everybody quietly did their own suffering in our place. It was every man for himself and the devil take the hind part. My brother Jerry always denied that there were any sores on any of us. He also denied that he was ever hungry. He must have been living in a different house is the way I figure it.

Even Jeyes Fluid, the stuff we used in the scrub water for the floors, did its turn as a medical remedy. One morning, when I was in grade five, I noticed red circular spots about the size of quarters covering my hands. I went to the bathroom and rolled up my sleeves.

My arms were also covered with the spots. I then opened the buttons on my uniform and saw that my entire chest was covered in the same angry-looking red spots. I was itching like crazy. Strangely enough, my face was spared.

I went back to class and got through until lunchtime. Then I raced home to Allan Square and hysterically showed my mother the spots. Now that I'm older and wiser, I think those spots were ringworm, but who really knows?

My mother obviously knew what the spots were. She didn't say anything, but told me to get the bottle of Jeyes Fluid from the shelf in the lobby.

I remember thinking, "My God! She expects me to scrub the floor in my condition? I should be in hospital, or at the very least, in bed. I'm sure I'm going to die. I'll never live to see fifteen."

I have no idea why I thought so, but I could have sworn I was going to pass on at the age of fifteen. Where that magical number came from I have no idea, but nobody seemed surprised to see me still around after my fifteenth birthday, except me.

Jerry had the same fixation, but he expected to die at thirty-seven, the same age our father had been when he died. For the rest of his life, every year after thirty-seven my brother treated as a bonus, not a bad way to look at life, actually.

My mother knocked the idea of me scrubbing the floor right out of my head when she told me to strip. She got a pail of warm water and poured in a liberal amount of the disinfectant. Fortunately for me I had developed a tolerance for the smell. In fact, I quite liked it.

She scrubbed me down so vigorously that I couldn't see the spots anymore. My whole body was as red as the spots had been. There was no rinse. I was told to put on my pyjamas and, after a bowl of soup, was advised to lie down and take a rest. I gladly fell on my cot and went out like a light, my nostrils stinging from the wafting aroma of Jeyes Fluid still clinging to my body. I was too exhausted to care. I slept right through the rest of the day and the night.

When I got up the next morning the spots were completely gone. It was like one of Jesus' miracles! I was allowed to stay home from school for the day. Mom wanted to be able to check for a return of the spots, I suppose, but they had gone away and they stayed away.

I was convinced then, and even now, that my mother, in

another time and place, could have had a great career in medicine. She raised us with practically nothing and we all survived. Except for the rotten teeth and a lingering craving for sweets, we didn't do that badly.

I don't know what they do nowadays for ringworm.

Chapter 27

I worshipped my mother's sister, my aunt and godmother. We all called her Kaddy and she was a very large part of my childhood for as long as I can remember. I spent a great deal of time in her house, days at a time.

They lived on Portugal Cove Road. Her kitchen, as I remember it, was always bright, cheerful and clean, clean, clean. It was painted a pale yellow and the window had white lace tieback curtains. I felt so special when she served me food, because a tablecloth was laid and it was so different from life on Allan Square. They were so generous to us after the death of my father, sharing everything they had. At Christmas they came with a beautifully prepared turkey, fully cooked. They also brought two homemade fruitcakes every year, one dark and the other light. The light one was my favourite.

My uncle's mother was also a beautiful woman, tall and stately, with snow-white hair tied back in a bun. She was a brilliant seamstress and made pyjamas, dresses and coats for me.

When her husband passed away, she made a long coat for my brother Jack from one of his wool overcoats. Jack was so pleased. He couldn't thank her enough. She asked him to say a prayer for her husband's soul whenever he wore the coat. Long after the coat was outgrown he prayed for her husband's soul every night when he went to bed.

I was very possessive of my Aunt Kaddy. She had cared for me a lot of the time after I was born because my mother was too sick. My aunt told me that when I began to talk I said, "You is my nice mommy!" I sincerely hope that my mother didn't hear me say it, but she probably did. If she did hear it that might explain the Judas comment when I approached to kiss her. (Like Judas, I also leaned in to kiss from the side.)

As I grew up, we remained close and she was always very loving to me. When my brothers and I got older we called her Aunt Kathy, which sounded a lot better than Kaddy, and I'm certain she appreciated the transition, but she never made a comment.

My uncle had a part-time job making deliveries by horse and sled. I don't remember what he was delivering, but I do know that whenever he was around our street all the kids piled on his sled for a ride around the block. It was great fun.

* * * * *

Inside my head, where I really lived, the foul language rolled around and around. As the indoctrination of religion began in earnest at school, I learned that a nightly Act of Contrition was the cure for the bad words. After reciting the Act of Contrition, I could wake up in the morning, cleansed and ready to begin a new day of silent cursing.

I visited the church after school every day, standing in the very back of the church, under a huge statue of the crucified Christ, who had suffered and died for my cursing, among other evils of the world. I gazed at the wound the Roman soldier's infamous spear had made in His side until I became dizzy and almost reached a state approaching rapture. By that time my eyes were playing tricks, and it looked like there were at least three or four crucified figures hanging from three or four Crosses. Just before I felt ready to fall, I finally staggered from the dimness of the church into the blinding sunlight. By this time I was in a state nearing sainthood and peacefully made my way down Garrison Hill, home to Allan Square.

The girls in the Presentation Convent went on retreats a number of times a year. They were usually three-day retreats. During this time we attended Mass on a morning basis and received communion. We were forbidden to talk during the retreats, and the school was indeed a silent place. The nuns were probably in raptures about the lovely silence. Mom had always been told when there was a retreat, and I must say, she respected my imposed silence. It was probably a great relief for her, too. I know it was for me. I never got in trouble during the retreats, at home or in school.

For the older people the church held three-day retreats known as the "Missions" – they were held at separate times for men and women. Silence was not mandatory for these.

Fire-and-brimstone Jesuits were brought to town and preached up a storm, decrying birth control and its evils and other matters that actually were none of their damn business. When I left school I attended these missions myself and cowered in my seat at the screaming of the preachers. It seemed the tougher the priests were, the more the women liked them.

One night at the mission, I met one of the neighbours from Allan Square.

"My! Look at you!" she gushed. "All grown up and at the women's mission! My God, how time does fly. You know, you were the most gorgeous little girl I ever laid eyes on in my life!"

She peered more closely into my face and delivered her *coup de grace* with relish.

"What in the name of the sweet, honourable Christ happened to you, anyway? You certainly lost all your looks."

I looked her straight in the face and walked away, swear words running through my head like crazy. Finally I went back to where she stood on the church steps, looked her straight in the eye and spewed out, "Fuck you! You ugly old bitch. You never had any good looks to lose!"

Her jaw dropped.

The Jesuits conducting the mission would have branded the both of us as heretics and used us as a topic for the next night's mission.

My outburst confirmed a fear I had. It was the reason I always sat as close to the back of the church as I could. I was terrified that, during some sermon or other, I would yell out some awful comment, maybe even spew out some of my colourful language.

A touch of Tourette's syndrome, maybe?

At the time I realized that such thinking was not quite normal, but what did I know about normal, anyway? My little corner of Allan Square was not exactly conducive to normality.

Another night I walked home from the mission behind two ladies, keeping close enough to overhear their comments. So I was nosy. Their voices carried very well, their St. John's Irish brogues were thick and colourful.

First lady: "Did ya hear that fella last night? He's some handsome! He could put his shoes under my bed any old night, so he could!"

Second lady: "Christ Almighty! He's some good, girl! Frightens the life out of ya, that's what he does, my dear!"

First lady: "Sure, he's right, ya know. The world is going to the dogs, that's fer sure!"

Second lady: "Nobody with a lick of common sense can deny that! Didn't ya just love his accent?"

First lady: "Them Mainlanders talks some grand, girl! I just loves listening to 'em meself, don't you?"

I grew bored and hurried on ahead.

My mom was never well enough to attend the missions, but my Aunt Kaddy did.

I could never imagine her having any sins to confess to a priest. She had no bad language in her vocabulary. I never heard her swear or use anything other than proper language. She had been a teacher for a while and commanded respect. Her husband, my sweet uncle, was as quiet as an old mouse. For all I know, they may have put the place up when they were alone, but never in front of company. It just wasn't done.

During a certain time of the year the church sent their priests out to collect the yearly dues or stipend; whatever could be afforded was fine with them. They probably did very well in the homes of the wealthy, but on Allan Square there were very few well-off Catholics, and that included our family.

During the period when the priest was expected to visit the street, my mother instructed me to sit on the doorstep and warn her when he was getting close to our place. She sat in the kitchen waiting as I answered the door and escorted him down the hall, through the lobby and into the kitchen.

The visit was always short. After my mother handed him her small offering, the priest beat a hasty retreat. My mother heaved a sigh of relief. She did not respond well to authority figures, which members of the clergy were in those days.

Personally, I always felt they should have given us some money, rather than taking some of the little we had. But, of course, it never happened that way.

I grovelled as I escorted him to the front door and slammed it behind him.

Chapter 28

Helen, Moll and I were the best of friends. Helen and I attended the Presentation Convent, and Moll the Mercy Convent. We chummed around together on a pretty regular basis, but Helen was more ladylike than Moll and I, except when she performed Salome's "Dance of the Seven Veils." Then all her dramatic flair blossomed, and her resemblance to the actress Susan Hayward became very pronounced.

We were usually in the vestibule of one of the girls on the street as we settled down for a performance. Moll and I tried to perform, but we just couldn't get our ungainly bodies around the sexy moves of the dance.

Helen, however, was something else again. She had every dance move down pat and did an amazing job of it. In a different life, with different advantages, she could have become a star. Her flaming red curly hair flowing around her pale face, blue eyes shining, she provided the background humming as she began her dance. Her arms slowly moved above her head until her hands were able to join. Her feet flew and her body moved in sways to her humming. We were almost brought to the doors of the harem. We were all transfixed.

The nuns would have been horrified, and we three would have been recommended for excommunication at the very least. Talk about going to forbidden movies!

Helen did not hang out with us on a regular basis. Her grandmother, with whom she lived, kept her on a very tight rein. Helen left Allan Square when she was in the ninth grade and went to live with her mother.

Moll and I loved Water Street on Saturdays. Going in and out of the stores, checking out the merchandise, was one of our favourite pastimes. When we reached McMurdo's Drugstore we stopped in for chips and gravy, our favourite treat. They always put dressing on the plate, and it was great!

We sized-up the counter area to see if there were any Yanks there and did a little staring. It was great fun. The Yanks usually noticed us and stared back. They were probably thinking that we were jailbait, but we were too innocent at the time to think about that. After feasting we started toward the west end of Water Street, again sizing up the Yanks and checking out their cute bums.

If the sidewalks were crowded, which they usually were on a Saturday, we called out in unison, "Hubba hubba! Give us some skin!" Those were the words of a popular wartime song, and we didn't have a clue as to what the words meant, but the Yanks did. They knew when chicks were coming on to them. By the time they got their bearings and turned around, Moll and I were calmly checking out a store window.

As soon as the Yanks moved away to continue along the street, we did it again. Same scenario. We got a great kick out of it, but the Yanks were only frustrated and ticked off.

Then we sang:

The Yankees thought they won the war,
Parlez-Vous!
The Yankees thought they won the war,
Parlez-Vous!
The Yankees thought they won the war, but the Newfies won it the year before.
Inkey Dinkey Parlez-Vous!

When the Yanks refused to acknowledge the two saucy brats tailing them, we got bored with their bums and turned up

Adelaide Street to Allan Square, where we never saw any Yanks. We did see, every now and then, Portuguese sailors from the White Fleet, whose fishing vessels were moored in the harbour. They wore baggy pants, not cute uniforms, and most of them were old enough to be our fathers. There was no scent of danger about them, and they never noticed us anyway. They were too busy kicking a ball around and were on their way to Bannerman Park, where they could really use up some energy in a serious ball game.

Every now and then, when Helen's grandmother was in a good mood, she would tell Helen that I could come upstairs and play with her. I jumped at the chance to play with another girl and to get away from my brothers for a time.

Helen's grandmother always sat in her rocking chair by the window. Her hair was snow white and she wore a long, black dress with a long, white-bibbed apron.

She was mumbling something to herself one day as Helen and I sat at the table playing with our cutouts. I listened carefully and realized she was counting on her fingers and naming names.

"There was wan and there was two and there was t'ree." She was counting her children, who were scattered all over the country. She was trying to remember them, and it made me sad.

One of us lightened the atmosphere by breaking wind. With that, the grandmother forgot her lost children and hoisted herself up from the rocking chair, moving slowly across the kitchen to answer the door.

"Who's there?" she shouted at the top of her lungs. Of course, nobody answered. Helen and I, wicked little buggers, doubled over with laughter until the tears began to flow. By this time, the grandmother had had enough. She glared at me from under her grey bushy brows and pointed to the door.

"Get to hell downstairs out of it, you saucy little snot! I don't trust you, you little bitch! Your mother is going to hear about what you're doing up here, and 'pon my soul to God, she'll hear it this night of our Lord, too. I can guarantee you that!"

She turned her attention to Helen. "And you! You little Antichrist! Get the hell to bed out of my sight or I'll have yer guts for garters, so I will. Jesus, Mary and Joseph! I'll swing fer ya! That I will!" Allan Square was a haven for people with short fuses.

I listened outside the door for a while before venturing down to my family's love nest. I hoped and prayed that Helen would survive to walk to school with me the next morning. Misery loved company in those days, too, and I was definitely not an exception to that rule.

When I got home my brother Jerry was waiting to put my hair in rags. I was in the choir at school, and we had a concert the next day. He liked me to look nice. He was a sweetheart.

"Sit down on the floor, duckie, and I'll curl your long, black hair." He put in the rags expertly, and the next morning I had lovely curls.

Helen survived the night and we walked to school together the next morning, trying unsuccessfully to understand the adults in our lives.

Helen was a good girl. She didn't bum money from the Yanks at the theatres, and she was horrified to find out what we were doing. She was not allowed to go out of the house after supper. If she'd joined us in our money-making venture, her grandmother would have killed her if she'd found out.

Moll and I would not have fared any better if we had been found out. Killing would probably have been merciful compared to what might have happened to us.

We gave up on panhandling after a while, anyway. We realized just how dangerous it was one evening when we saw a neighbour in the lineup. The sighting signalled the end of that budding enterprise. The neighbour never told anyone, as far as we knew. Perhaps she hadn't even noticed us, but we decided it was too risky to take any more chances.

After the sighting we counted our blessings and our little bit of cash and straggled home to Allan Square. We both agreed that the experience, fraught with danger as it had been, was well worth it. The sense of forbidden activity was heady, and the Yanks were sure not short of cash.

After school every day we played skipping games, hopscotch, marbles and "H'ist Yer Sails and Run" or "Hide and Go Seek." We also played "Nicky Nicky Nine Doors." We knocked on doors all over the block and then ran like hell. We threw stink bombs into people's halls. God! They stank like hell. Nowadays we would be arrested as juvenile delinquents.

After the stink bombs, we didn't run; we usually sat on a nearby step, looking innocent and pointing: "They went that way" when the owner struggled through the door gasping and choking for air. Who in their right mind would suspect two little convent girls of doing such a dastardly thing? Obviously nobody did, because we never once got caught.

I must say that Helen, God love her, never participated in any of our mischief. She simply danced for her own entertainment and pleasure. She believed her grandmother's threats of death. Moll and I also took the threats as gospel. The poor old dear was a fearsome sight when she ventured out of the house to search for Helen if the child dared to leave Allan Square. Granny had the vocabulary of a drunken sailor, but she didn't shock me with any of her swearing. I'd heard and digested worse than anything she could spit out. Just the same, we all lived in fear when we saw her coming.

When I happened to be alone, I sometimes played hopscotch on the corner of Allan Square and Queen's Road.

One day I looked up and saw one of the neighbourhood men making his way up Theatre Hill. He was impeccably dressed in a brown suit and quiff hat, but with my usual eye for liquor, I sensed that he had taken in a few ales. He walked straight as an arrow, a bit too straight for the incline of that hill. So I stopped hopping to watch.

He also stopped and simply stared at me. Then he

melted me, right in my tracks. For the first and last time in my life, I watched a man remove his hat and tip it to me. I suddenly felt so grown-up and respectable. Men, as far as I knew, only tipped their hats to ladies.

I definitely had the makings of a lady. I was not a slut, as my mother frequently called me.

A slut would not have had a man tip his hat to her, unless he was one desperate man.

I was going to be a lady when I grew up, an earthy one, maybe, but a bona-fide lady nonetheless. I went home pleased and happy. I didn't give a shit what anyone called me from that time on. Well, maybe I did care about the nuns, a lot. They had thick straps to enforce their opinions.

For the most part, though, I trusted instead in a well-dressed man of obvious good taste, a man who recognized a lady when he saw one.

So what if she happened to be playing hopscotch at the time?

Respect. It was the first time I had received any, and it felt wonderful. He shines in my memories.

Chapter 29

While it was generally fire and brimstone at the church-sponsored missions, this was not totally true in our flat. We did have our peaceful times; it was not constant misery, although my mother definitely enjoyed fighting with me. A strange fact, but true.

Sometimes in the evenings Jack and I sat before the Ideal coal range in the dark kitchen and listened to Mom tell ghost stories from her home in Bonavista Bay.

Storytelling was an art in those days. We had no TV, and not much in the way of entertainment. After the ghost yarns Jack often pulled out his harmonica and played us a tune. Those were nice times. Bob didn't really like to sit still and listen to stories, so he was rarely present. He was usually out hanging around with his friends.

Other evenings a group of our friends would gather on our doorstep, and we would sing songs and tell more ghost stories. Those times were fun and normal. I enjoyed the respite.

Bob's teeth had to be removed also. He had a very difficult time of it. Clots of blood as big as pieces of liver oozed from his mouth, and his face was as white as a sheet. Finally my stepfather could take it no more. He raced out the hall and into the front room where Bob was lying in bed, holding blood-soaked towels to his face. Without any more ado, my stepfather, who was a powerfully built man, scooped Bob up into his arms and took him out the front door to the car. He whipped him right along to the hospital for emergency treatment. If he hadn't acted so quickly, poor Bob would not have had a chance.

They returned about three hours later. Bob's mouth was packed with dressings, and he looked like a chipmunk. The bleeding had stopped, and I felt a sense of respect for and gratitude toward my stepfather. He loved Bob, who was the baby of the family, and took him back regularly to have the packing changed, until Bob was fully recovered. It was a close shave, and my mother was eternally grateful to my stepfather for stepping up to the plate when he was needed. We all were grateful.

My stepfather was in his sane, sober senses at that time. He had not taken a drink since that cure in the mental hospital. He and my mother still had their upsets, but nothing like the ones I had called the police for. I just knew that they were mad at each other, but not why. Then the next day they were suddenly the best of buddies again, talking to each other as if nothing at all had ever been wrong. I was totally mystified at what could have happened overnight to suddenly cause such peace in the house. I was a bit thick, obviously, and certainly not aware of the beneficial effect of sexual healing.

I guess I didn't really need to know everything.

* * * * *

The year my oldest brother returned from his tour of duty in Germany, I was in the middle of the first term of my last year in high school. In those days we finished at grade eleven, unless one wanted to go on to do the secretarial course. It was called "Commercial" and included all the skills needed for an office career.

One night I was doing homework in the kitchen when I heard my mother's voice from the bedroom. It sounded strange, slurred and slow. I opened their bedroom door and immediately saw that there was something wrong with her. Her mouth was twisted and her eyes filled with panic. She could not move the left side of her body.

We still had no telephone, so I woke my stepfather, and he quickly dressed and went to look for a doctor. I had no idea where he was going to find one, because by this time it was about two-thirty in the morning.

He came back about half an hour later with a tall, sleepy doctor trailing in his wake. He was the police doctor and my stepfather had, in fact, found him at the police station. The doctor had a thick Scottish brogue and, after a cursory examination, declared that my mother was suffering from "hysterics."

He gave her some kind of shot, and she settled down to sleep. The next morning there was no change. She still had no movement on her left side. My stepfather left to find another doctor, who came and quickly ordered an ambulance, declaring that my mother had suffered a paralytic stoke. She was taken to the hospital and remained there for a couple of weeks.

I had absolutely no idea of how to care for a stroke victim. We had a nurse from the Victorian Order of Nurses come in to care for her initially. I sat in on each session and learned the type of care that was crucial to someone in Mom's condition. I learned how to change the bed with her in it and how to wash her. She also needed daily alcohol rubs to prevent bedsores. She needed nourishing food, and I was no great cook, but I did my feeble best. It is to her credit that she initially held down everything I fed her, even the ever-present lumps in her Cream of Wheat.

Jerry, God love him, stayed with her when I went back to school. With the approval of my teacher I arrived late and left early, in order to take care of Mom. Jerry made pies to tempt her appetite. I saw first-hand why she had always referred to him as her Rock. I worshipped him.

But he had to get on with his life and look for work. I decided to leave school and go to night school to continue my grade eleven. Nobody, including my teacher, wanted me to do that, but I couldn't handle the pressure of school all day and then looking after my mom.

So I applied for night school and was accepted. It

turned out to be a whole new world for me. For one thing, it was co-ed. There were guys there, some of them very cute. There were older people, and people my age. I much preferred it to my previous all-girl environment. The change proved to be a smooth transition. I remember only one person from my grade eleven class at night school. He was blond, tall and really cute, and he seemed to like me. That was a change.

I had never been on a date before, and I was really surprised when he asked me if I would like to go to a movie with him. My sense of self-esteem was so low that I could see absolutely no reason at all why he should find me attractive. Poor little bitch!

He asked for my phone number, and I confessed that we didn't have a phone. He looked surprised at that but accepted it pretty well.

Anyway, I gave him my address, and we arranged a time for the pick-up. He didn't have a car, but he arrived on time and we walked to the Capitol Theatre, where Moll and I had done our bumming from the Yanks. I don't remember which movie we saw, but we didn't hold hands. He was very circumspect, even a little shy. Just like me. As a matter of fact, I was scared to death. The evening seemed to be going pretty well, though. I should have known something would happen to screw it up. It didn't take long, either.

We walked back to my place, which was, in fact, just up around the corner from the theatre. I guess we talked, but I don't remember.

When we arrived at the house, I couldn't figure out what to do next. There was a pole with a street light just outside my door, so I didn't feel like standing there with him and saying what I figured would be a public good night. Therefore, foolishly, I invited him just inside the front door, to the hall which held the washroom. I prayed that he wouldn't ask to use it; there was no light in there. Conditions were absolutely primitive. There was also no light in the hall. I could tell that he was just working up enough nerve to kiss me. I hadn't had a kiss since the usher days at the theatre, and I was waiting in anticipation. If he was expecting any help from me, he was shit out of luck. I was, God only knows why, the original frozen lady, and absolutely stunted in matters of social growth. I suppose that's what arrested development really means.

Just as I felt his hands groping in the dark, trying to find my shoulders, we were both shocked when a light flashed. The kitchen door opened, and I saw my stepfather framed in the doorway. He was holding a broom in his hand. It was eleven o'clock in the night, and I wondered what in the hell he was going to sweep at this godforsaken hour. Every other night by that time he was usually out like a light under the watchful eyes of St. Thérèse.

He vigorously swept down the steps leading from the kitchen and continued sweeping out the lobby to the door to the hall. That door had a little glass panel down one side, and I watched in fascination and horror as the dust rose and shimmered, backlit by the light from the kitchen. The lobby had no light either, so I knew that my "date" would not be able to see my blushing face. I thanked God for small mercies. Something told me that I would not be going on another date with this charming young man. He appeared much too sensible for that.

My stepfather continued to work his way through the lobby, sweeping corners that hadn't seen a broom in years. The dust was rising, and he started to cough just as he reached the hall door.

As my stepfather was yanking open the door, my young gentleman caller, faint of heart and no doubt wishing he was anywhere but in my hall, blindly reached for the doorknob and pulled at it.

"You have to turn it." I whispered, and he did just that, mumbling good night as he awkwardly ran down the steps. I watched him hightail it up the street. By this time my stepfather had ensconced himself in the washroom. I silently hoped that the miserable old bastard's ass would freeze to the porcelain toilet and that he'd never be able to get off. Would serve him right. Still, I guess when you gotta go, you gotta go, and it doesn't matter who's in the hall trying to say good night and steal a kiss.

After that first disastrous attempt at romance, the young man and I both acted as if it had never happened. We continued our school year as strangers in the night.

He never asked me out again, and I stopped blushing after a while.

* * * * *

My mother managed to keep her spirits up when she was bedridden after her stroke. I think fighting with me helped her a lot. She seemed to need someone on the other end of an argument.

Now that my stepfather was sober, she couldn't really pick a fight with him; he might not have responded. She never, as far as I can remember, fought with any of my brothers. I, however, was so used to being picked on that I considered it the normal way to live.

I have to admit that I was mouthy and didn't take the abuse lying down. I would have had to be dead to be able to take it. My mother was very proprietary about our fights. They were strictly between us. She yelled at one of my brothers once when he had the temerity to interfere in one of our spats.

"Leave her alone! That's enough! I don't want her spirit broken! She's going to need her spirit!"

I remember wondering at the time if she was clairvoyant and foresaw some awful future for me that included terrible things. She did take up for me that time, though, and that was heartwarming. I was pathetically easy to please. I didn't really forgive my brother for quite a while; I don't respond well to physical violence. He probably doesn't even remember the episode at all.

Anyway, I had a break in the evenings when I went to night school. I took the CHE exams that year and passed. The exams were set by the Council of Higher Examinations in England and were standard in every high school across

Newfoundland. They were sent to England for marking. I met up with some of my former schoolmates from the Presentation each day after the exams; we compared notes and commiserated with each other. It actually felt good to be with the girls again. Normal in fact.

In the meantime, I was not too bad at caring for my mother. I can say that I did my best. She got a kick out of my sense of humour. I could break her up on the spot with a smutty joke or even a facial expression, so much so that one day she warned me, "Don't you dare make me laugh when I'm dying!"

Talk about mixed signals!

The next year I went back to night school and enrolled in the Commercial Program. I learned to type, which I hated, and I learned to take shorthand, which I also hated. I managed to scrape a pass. I joined the Catholic Youth Club. Every second Catholic couple in St. John's had met a spouse there over the years.

My brother Lew returned to the scene and bought my mother a TV. That enriched her life to a large degree. He also bought her a refrigerator, a nice modern convenience. It meant the jelly did not have to go outside to set.

At night school I was not exactly looked upon by the guys as chopped liver. I had been asked out a couple of times. Several fellows wanted my phone number. My stepfather insisted that the old house did not have the wiring required to support a phone. That was a load of bunk. Before he knew what was happening, the phone was hooked up in the kitchen. It was a party line. In the phone book it was listed under my name. The phone was a nice diversion for my mother. It meant she had contact with the outside world. She could call her favourite sister whenever she felt like it.

I have to admit my mom had spunk and fire galore in her spirit. She also had a mighty sharp way with her tongue of delivering not-too-subtle insults, most of them directed at me. Every now and then I lay down beside her on the bed, just for company. If I turned over she muttered, "Beached whale!"

That comment did its job well and was intended strictly for that purpose. It made me feel like a big, fat, clumsy cow. I swallowed it, as usual.

My mother was about five-one and I was five-seven, so there was no way I was able to feel petite and dainty around her.

I'm sure she wondered how, in the name of all that was holy, she had ever produced such a giant of a daughter. I remembered the captain marching us around the auditorium during my convent days, and I recited his words to myself regularly. "Head up! Shoulders back! Tummy in! Chest out!"

To hell with everybody if they couldn't take my height and my build: I was determined they would never be able to find fault with my posture.

My mother's relatives, when they came to town for a doctor's appointment, always dropped in for a visit. The comment upon seeing me was, "Isn't she a handsome girl!"

They meant no harm; girls were often called handsome in those days. I would have preferred to be called pretty, thank you very much.

For the life of me I cannot recall how the arguments between my mother and me started.

If the "beached whale" comment was not enough to start one, I can't imagine another comment from her that would have aroused a response in me. Something started them, that's all I can say with certainty.

One day she was sitting in her rocker wearing a colourful Japanese kimono that my brother Jack had brought home to her when he returned from the Army. He was laden with gifts for everyone, God love him.

I was reading at the kitchen table and stealing glances at her as she stared out the window into the backyard. She looked so pretty with her lovely blue eyes, and she appeared so sad. I remember pitying her because of the stroke and thinking how unfair it was, after the hard life she'd lived.

The next thing I knew, up she blew! A mother of a fight ensued, with both of us yelling at each other.

Personally, although I had not heard of him at the time, I was like the comedian Rodney Dangerfield. I didn't get no respect, no how, no time. I had learned not to expect it.

Another day, when she and I were calm and companionable, she suddenly said to me, "I want you to promise me something."

That got my attention fast, and I looked at her questioningly, waiting for the rest.

"I want you to promise me!" She spoke in a grave tone. "When something happens to me." We both knew what she meant. "I want you to get out of this house right away. No waiting around, no talking to anyone about it. I want you to promise that you'll take your few things and get as far away as fast as you can from Allan Square!"

My blood ran cold at the gravity of her tone. Naturally, I asked about her reasons for saying it, but she gave no response, simply repeated her order and made me promise, once and for all, to do as she said.

I guess I must have had a silly smile on my face after her little talk.

She looked at me hopelessly and said sternly, "For God's sake, girl! What do you have to be so shit-happy about? Wipe that stupid smile off your face. This is serious talk here."

So I wiped away the smile.

Chapter 30

There were two things that were never spoken to me or by me, when I was growing up on Allan Square. Unless of course, one considered the nightly "Act of Contrition" – and that simply reinforced the guilt-ridden parts of my personality.

One unspoken phrase was "I love you."

The other was "I'm sorry."

There was no way my mother would accept or even hear of "I'm sorry."

There was no way I could ever consider saying to my mother "I love you."

Nor did she ever use the words on me. I guess in those days, emotions were kept under close wraps.

For all I knew, maybe nobody but courting couples expressed their love openly and freely. Passion has a way of blasting emotions to the surface.

I know that Moll and Helen experienced the same thing. Helen said to me years later, "It was terrible growing up with no love." The word "love" was not bandied about in Moll's home, either.

Maybe the adults were too tired and too busy scraping out a living to have any time for heavy emotions when it came to their offspring.

So there were three little girls, each of us starved for two simple emotions: love, which breeds tenderness and security, and regret, which breeds forgiveness and nurtures love.

Because of the volatile nature of my relationship with my mother, there was no shortage of sins to confess to the dark figure behind the confessional screen.

On the way to weekly confession, I tortured myself all the way up the steep steps of Garrison Hill to the massive cathedral on Harvey Road. The sins came readily to the surface of my mind as I sat on the hard wooden bench, waiting my turn to be forgiven.

If my mother wouldn't or couldn't give me forgiveness, I knew that the priest on the other side of the wooden box would not hesitate. He might lecture me, but because he couldn't see my face, I knew he wouldn't recognize me in a police lineup or anywhere else.

"Bless me, Father, for I have sinned." The words came out by rote. "It has been one week since my last confession."

"I had bad thoughts." I was never asked for details. Bad, in the parlance of the convent, signified "impure."

I guess he figured from my youthful voice that I was not out screwing half the Americans at Fort Pepperrell, so that sin was passed over quickly. No details called for or given.

"I talked back to my mother and gave her grief." That did wake him up, and a short lecture ensued, during which he dwelt on the importance of giving respect to one's mother.

"Your mother, my child, deserves all your respect. Try to do better in the future. Your mother gave you the greatest gift she could. She gave you life."

I could tell from the tone of his voice that he was becoming impatient and needed to be talking to someone a little more stimulating than a mind-numbing child.

"Is there anything else?"

I answered in the negative, neglecting to mention that I had gone into Protestant churches, and bummed money from servicemen. I was very selective about sin in those days.

I waited expectantly, listening to the rattle of his rosary beads as he lifted his hand to give me absolution.

"Go in peace. Your sins are forgiven." Or words to that

effect – they were in Latin – but they stilled my soul nevertheless.

The forgiveness denied by my mother poured down in a healing balm on my sinful head.

Usually I was given ten Hail Marys and ten Our Fathers for penance.

I then habitually walked through the church and knelt at the cold, marble altar rail, reciting my penance by rote. I stared at the statue of the Sacred Heart, who had suffered and died for my sins. I felt genuine regret, mingled with a deep sense of relief.

I thought about other sins that I had committed during the week, and I forgave myself on the spot. After all, I couldn't help it if I was not able to banish my stepfather's curse words from my mind. Therefore, they did not constitute "grievous matter, wilful knowledge and full consent."

I decided that any transgressions I had not confessed just did not meet the criteria set by the Church for sin, and I stepped out into the blinding sunlight, forgiven for another week.

The next morning I attended nine o'clock Mass, where I sang in the school choir. I felt so holy when I walked to the altar that I felt like floating. It was probably partly hunger, because in those days one fasted from the previous night before taking communion.

The nuns always said denial was good for the soul, but I had serious doubts about that, especially when it involved food.

When I felt my eyes cross on the way down the aisle from communion, I said to myself, "Head for home, girl, and get something to eat."

I could always confess the next week that I had skipped out early from Mass. What could the priest do, anyway? I brushed the entire matter from my mind and rushed home for tea and toast.

Remembering the priest's words from the confessional, about my debt to my mother for giving me life, I made some tea and toast for my mother as well. In an attempt to forestall an argument, I passed on making her any of my lumpy Cream of Wheat.

"Sufficient onto the day is the evil thereof."

There were times when I definitely didn't think it wise to rock the boat. If lumpy cereal caused a fight in our kitchen, then I simply removed it from the menu and pretended I had forgotten to make it. I still can't make Cream of Wheat without lumps, even the instant stuff. I just can't seem to get my mind and my stirring hand in sync. It's a carry-over from Allan Square, I figure.

My kids never complained to me about the lumps, though, but none of them really cared much for Cream of Wheat.

Speaking of lumps, now that I think of it, I also made lumpy gravy. Great gobs of white floating in a sea of gravy, which was almost black from the addition of liquid browning, did absolutely nothing to tempt my mother's delicate appetite.

In the early days after my mother's stroke, she had to depend on me to make and bring her meals. It must have been really difficult for a woman who, in her heyday, had been an absolutely brilliant cook, one who could put on a tasty meal with what seemed to be little effort.

Here was her only daughter, big enough and ugly enough, and she was still unable to provide her mother with a tasty bite of food.

Finally she broke one day and said to me, after a particularly tasteless lunch, "Jesus, Mary and Joseph! When in the name of Christ are you ever going to learn to cook a bit of food properly? 'Pon my soul to God, girl! If you were working for me I'd have to fire you!"

It was on the tip of my tongue and the words almost slipped out, "If I was working in this place I'd have no choice but to quit!"

In my own defence, I can honestly say that I was not entirely useless in the kitchen. I made superb chocolate fudge.

As my mom reiterated, "Absolutely zero nutritional value!"

Since there was nobody else to do it, I had no choice. I continued trying to cook.

Time after time I turned out pea soup that had the consistency of gruel. The dumplings were hard as a rock. Mom's dumplings had always been light as a feather. The stewing meat rivalled the dumplings, as far as toughness was concerned. My stomach began building a rock when I even thought of cooking.

Mom had a friend who worked in the kitchen at Frost's restaurant on Harvey Road. She was so desperate for some tasty food that she often sent me up there to pick up a meal and a piece of coconut cream pie. She got the meals at the same price the staff paid and her friend often refused to take any money at all.

Things got a little easier for me in the kitchen after that. Her sister also helped, often arriving with blancmange and other titbits to tempt her appetite.

Between the jigs and the reels she survived, thank God.

At least I didn't have to risk the priest's ire in the confessional by having to tell him my lousy cooking was starving my mother to death.

My guilt-ridden conscience could only carry so much sin.

Chapter 31

Not all the memories of Allan Square are tales of misery and woe. There was not much money floating around, though. I remember each year my mother gave me a dollar to go to the drugstore and buy a jar of Pond's Cold Cream. That was my Christmas present to her.

One year for Christmas I got a pair of white skates. I was absolutely thrilled and enjoyed them enormously. Even when they got too small for me, I still forced my feet into them and skated freely down the steep length of Long's Hill. There were no helmets in those days. It's a wonder I didn't kill myself. The hill ran down to the corner of Queen's Road and looked like a small mountain to me. I should have really been using skis; it would have been safer.

My stepfather's sister – the one who worked at the biscuit factory and kept us supplied – turned up every Christmas, laden with gifts. There was always an elaborate pencil box for me, and a reversible, satin comforter for my mother's bed.

"It's no more than she should do, the old bitch!" My mother was totally unappreciative.

"She should get down on her hands and knees to me for taking the son of a bitch off her hands!"

One year, along with the gifts, my aunt brought a large bag of biscuits and chocolates. Tucked away in the bottom of the bag was a pair of white fake fur mittens for me. I loved them, but the smell of biscuits actually turned my stomach. The mittens reeked. I had actually become sick of the smell of sweet biscuits. Imagine that! I never thought to see the day when that would happen. I kept the mittens away from my face as best I could and tried not to inhale.

Moll, Helen and I never exchanged gifts. Neither one of us had two cents to rub together. We all stayed at home on Christmas Day, enjoying the relative peace and traditional goodwill of the season.

Boxing Day and the entire week after Christmas became ours, and we took full advantage of it. We were not like the mummers who roamed certain parts of town in disguise and enjoyed the hospitality of any and all who would let them step inside the front door.

We went out, all right, but we were not in disguise at all. We went out as three cute little girls who still believed in the Christmas spirit. We usually stayed in our own environs. If a house had a decorated Christmas tree in the window, it was fairly safe to assume the spirit of Christmas would settle upon us as soon as our knock was heard. It rarely failed.

"Mister, could we see your tree, please?"

We took turns making the request. Only a person with no heart could have refused us. We weren't asking for the moon, but we were expecting a glass of syrup, a piece of cake and maybe a few chocolates.

We also sincerely loved looking at decorated trees.

Sometimes it would be an older couple who lived in the house. A few times nobody answered our knock, but we knew someone was at home because we could hear music and laughter from inside. We chalked up the rejection to experience and moved on down the street. A faint heart would never get any syrup or other goodies. We were cock-eyed optimists!

One time a little old lady answered the door. There was a beautifully decorated tree in her window. She was a sweet little old lady with a lovely smile. She opened her door and gestured us inside.

"You three remind me of myself when I was your age." She said, "Sure, myself and my friends used to do the very same thing as you're doing now. Sit down, now, my darlings, and I'll get you a bite to eat."

We sat politely on the sofa and waited patiently for the lady to return.

She came back into the front room with a silver tray laden with goodies – cookies, slices of fruitcake and squares. There was also a crystal dish filled with chocolates. We knew it was crystal, because Helen later told us her granny had one exactly like it. The lady laid the tray on the table and returned to the kitchen. When she came back she had another silver tray with doilies and wine glasses. There were two jugs of syrup as well, one strawberry and one orange.

We were awed by the service and her attitude toward us. This was obviously a woman of some breeding. She encouraged us to remove our coats, and then she hung them in the hall on a darkly shining wooden coat rack. There was a fire blazing in the black marble fireplace. She gave the fire a sharp root with the poker and laid on some more wood. Then she sat across from us and put her feet up on a hassock, watching us expectantly as we went to work on the goodies.

We put on our best manners, because she deserved it, as far as we were concerned. We delicately brushed the crumbs away with the napkins she had provided and listened to her reedy voice as she talked about "Mister," who had been dead for five years.

"'Pon my soul to God, girls, I still expect himself to walk through the front door any time of the day or night. I know he's still with me. I can feel his presence all the time. You know, we were together for fifty years, and not a chick nor child in all that time. It was sad; we could have provided a child with a good home, you know. But if it's not in God's plans, then we have nothing to do but respect His will. God love him and rest his sweet soul; sure, he used to lie for his nap on that very settee you three are sitting on."

She pointed to the shiny black leather couch and her eyes misted over. We revelled in being there and keeping her company, but we were a bit leery at the thought that "Mister" could be sitting right on the couch with us.

Then her natural curiosity came to life. She asked each one of us where we lived and our names. As we answered in turn, she asked each one of us a question.

"Now, my child," she said to me, "Murphy, you say. Well, that's certainly a St. John's name."

She peered at me intently. "Now, who are you one of?" I was a bit puzzled. She saw that and said, "I mean, what's your father's name and your mother's? Where are they from? How old are you and what school do you go to? Where do you live?"

This was getting dangerous. She might know someone we were related to. God knows, maybe even Helen's granny. We stared at each other in apprehension and prepared to bolt.

The interrogation continued until she must have had enough information to fill out a C.I.D. report. Their own detectives could not have done better.

By the time she finished pulling the information from us, we were exhausted and began to think about getting out of there. Mister's portrait was staring gravely at us from the wall behind her chair, and he looked a bit spooky. The Sacred Heart was bleeding profusely from the wound in His side on the other wall.

Besides, the food was all gone and the fire was dying.

Suddenly, she put us out of our misery when she stood up, leaning heavily on her cane.

"Well now, my loves, I suppose it's time for you three to be making your way home. It's getting dark, and your people will be worried about where you are."

She got our coats and handed them to us, watching carefully as we buttoned them up and put on our hats.

She admired Helen's flaming red hair and kissed each of us on the cheek. We were overcome by her kindness.

Outside the snow was glistening on the ground and more was beginning to fall heavily in large flakes.

She stood framed in her doorway, waving to us. We heard her voice thanking us for spending the time with her.

"Now! Straight home! Don't talk to any strangers. Don't worry about me. I've got my niece coming over for supper, and she's spending the night. She does that two or three times a week. I'm fine. God bless the three of you. You gave an old woman a bit of company and a lovely afternoon. I hope the three of you get good husbands! Merry Christmas to you all and a Happy New Year!"

On the way home we forgot about the goodies we'd consumed, and instead we talked about the old lady's sweetness, her beautiful manners, her cultured voice, her fine furniture, and the very sincere sense of welcome we had felt in her house.

Moll asked, in a very grown-up manner, "I wonder who she's one of?"

Later in the week our Christmas visitations went from the sublime to the ugly. Helen was busy that day, so Moll and I went out on our own. The last house we hit on the last day of the week was in stark contrast to the afternoon we had spent with the lovely little old lady. As a matter of fact, it ended our fun of turning up cold and brazenly asking to look at the Christmas trees of strangers.

The house we visited was on a side street north of Allan Square. It was a bit out of our usual comfort zone, but drawn by the lighted tree in the window, we knocked on the door anyway.

It was answered by a large man with a big gut hanging out over his belt. His white hair straggled over his forehead, and a pair of black wire glasses perched on his bulbous nose.

He peered intently at us over the glasses and demanded, "Yes?"

Moll chirped up, "Mister, could we please see your Christmas tree?"

He looked slightly surprised but called over his shoulder at someone we figured was his wife. God pity her, I thought to myself, whoever she was.

"Mag!" he bellowed. "Dere's two youngsters here who wants to see the friggin' Christmas tree. Do ya want me to let the little buggers in?"

"Yes b'y! Let 'em in, for Christ's sake, and for the love and honour of God, shut the damn door. I'm freezin' me ass off here!"

By this time the two little buggers were getting red alerts from built-in antennas. He sounded just a bit too much like the drunk assholes we were accustomed to on Saturday nights. But we couldn't smell the telltale stink of booze, stale or otherwise, so we snuck through the front door and carefully sidled past him.

We did not take off our coats, nor were we invited to do so.

His wife, a large woman in a faded housedress, sat warming her toes by the fireplace. Her feet were swollen out of shape. She looked exhausted and not very pleasant. As a matter of fact she looked crooked as sin. She had no teeth at all. Her white hair was kept in place by a fine hairnet.

I thought to myself, at least there'll be no hair in the fruitcake.

There was a small end table by the side of her chair. It held a glass half filled with sherry or wine. There was also a patterned china plate with the remnants of a piece of fruitcake. Resting on the plate beside the cake was a set of false teeth.

Her husband simply stood in the door to the front room, looking from us to her.

She sized us up and finally said, "Well, I s'pose ye wants a drop of syrup and a piece of cake or somethin', do ye?"

She picked up the set of false teeth and popped them into her mouth. With an obvious effort she hoisted herself up from the chair and slowly headed through the French doors into the kitchen.

"Wait right dere an' I sees what we got left. I 'low I'll dredge up somethin' fer ye, a drop of syrup an' a piece of cake, I dare say. Sit down on the couch, fer God's sake, ye looks like two frightened rabbits. We're not goin' ta eat ya up, never fear!"

I immediately sized the two of them up as being characters straight out of Dickens. Their house was fairly modern, though, and not in too bad a shape, compared to Allan Square anyway.

I was listening to the rattle of dishes and the running of water from the kitchen when Moll suddenly gave me an elbow in the side. I looked at her, and she indicated the door of the front room with her eyes.

There was mister, large as life and twice as ugly. He was standing with one eye on us and the other on the kitchen door. His pants zipper was down and his "thing," stiff and straight as a soldier on early morning roll call, was plainly visible to us. He had a pleased smile on his face and looked very proud of his erection. It was probably the first one he'd had in years.

Moll and I were of the same mind, and we nearly knocked the old pervert down when we rushed past him to the front door. He hurriedly pulled up his zipper and shouted to his wife. "Mag! Dem two little snots are leavin' after dey put ya to all dat work! How in Christ's name would I know wat's de matter wit' 'em? Da little divils are boltin' tru de door dis very minute!"

From our elocution classes at the convent we realized this was definitely an uncultured man, and he seemed to be what my mother would have referred to as "intyre-breed" – meaning the lowest of the low.

His front door was ajar and he just stood there backlit with a sick smile on his pasty face watching us as we high-tailed it away from his house.

When we figured we were far enough away from him, we turned around and started shouting at the top of our lungs.

I screamed, "Go inside, you dirty old bastard! Show your filthy old dick to someone who wants to see it!"

"You're going straight to hell, that's what you are!" Moll was crying as she screamed at him.

She said to me, "Sweet God! Is that like the thing some man is going to stick up into us when we grows up?"

We promised each other as we plodded home that we would never again go looking at Christmas trees in strange homes. We had learned that you never did know what you might see. Literally, it was a hard awakening for us.

No amount of syrup, no amount of fruitcake or chocolates, would ever again make it worthwhile.

It was a sad ending to what had become one of our sweet, innocent Christmas traditions.

Neither of us had ever seen a man's penis before up close and personal, so to speak. As a matter of fact, we didn't even know the word "penis." We called that part of a man's anatomy his "dickey bird." There were no sex-education classes at the convents.

Too bad the first adult one we saw was so ugly, but then again, maybe they were all ugly. What did we know?

We thought about it but decided against reporting him to the cops. That would do us no good at all. It would only get us in trouble. We simply decided not to go within an English mile of his house. If we ever chanced to see the dirty old bastard again, it was decided that we would run like hell and scream like banshees, or at the very least cross over to the other side of the street.

We swore each other to secrecy and dodged home to our beds and to the sleep of the innocent. I didn't even say my usual Act of Contrition that night.

The sin was not mine.

Chapter 32

My mother was a gutsy woman most of the time, but when she was in fighting mode she was really gutsy, and she showed her formidable temper at the drop of a hat.

One morning, when I was already grown up and out to work, we had the most frightening fight of all. As usual, I cannot remember what I did to cause her rage. Maybe I have a permanent block about all those reasons for the fights.

Anyway, she was in bed and I was getting ready to go to work. I was wearing a sleeveless blouse. It must have been a close confrontation, because she had no trouble reaching me. Before I knew what was happening, her face contorted with a rage I had never seen before, and I glimpsed what looked like hatred in her eyes.

She suddenly reached over with her good arm and swiftly gripped the paralyzed one. I had absolutely no time to react. She used the bad arm as a weapon and dragged her hand and nails fiercely down over my arm, from shoulder to wrist. The attack – because that's what it was – left deep scratch marks on my arm and drew blood. I was shocked, and she looked satisfied. That finished the argument. I changed the blouse for a long-sleeved sweater and left for work with the tears stinging my eyes. I wondered – not that I was anything remotely resembling a saint – what in the name of Christ I had done or said to bring forth such fury.

When I went home at lunchtime, it was as if nothing

had happened. If I hadn't seen the blood, I might have thought I was imagining things.

She often talked about her death to me. This depressed the hell out of me, but it also brought to the surface the fear of that very thing. That fear was always lurking in my subconscious anyway, but I didn't need it staring me in the face. Apparently the doctor had told her the next stroke would be her last one and that it could happen any time.

She said, "I'm so glad that I have a clean disease. There's usually no wasting away of the body with heart trouble."

So she prepared for it and lived with it. No wonder she was in a bad mood every now and then. She had to have something to take her mind away from her health. I was that something.

Mom had a blue and grey skirt that was part of a two-piece outfit, and she absolutely hated the material in that skirt. It was itchy and stiff. She called it her "bed-tick" skirt.

She decided she would wear the bed-tick skirt in her coffin. That was all it was fit for, she said.

"I'll wear my lovely pale blue blouse with it," she informed me. "You know, the one with the long sleeves that you bought for me at Bowrings. You make sure there's no hair on my face. Use the stuff you and Moll use, that Neet, or whatever the devil it's called. I won't feel it anyway. But I don't want people staring down at me and counting the hairs on my face. You know how people get up close and personal when they're looking into a coffin at a corpse."

Although I didn't tell her, I knew all about it. I had stared into many a casket in my young life.

"You wash me and get me ready. I don't want any undertaker seeing me in my figure, with no clothes on!"

I listened in silence. I already knew that I would be in no shape to prepare her for viewing when the time came.

There were fresh nylons, underwear, and shoes all laid out neatly in a drawer. She calmly showed me where everything was kept in the wardrobe. I found it to be a harrowing discussion and so matter-of-fact. I wondered where she got the nerve to face her own demise like that. But face it she did, and she forced me to face it as well. I think that may well have been the object of the whole exercise.

The very thought of her dying sent me into a state of panic.

She did not want to be waked in a funeral home. That was beginning to be the trend in St. John's. Wakes held in the deceased's home were destined to be a thing of the past, but she wanted a wake at home and she held me to the promise. When the time came, I would see to it.

I promised.

"We'll put the casket between the windows! Perfect! Make sure I have my lipstick on. Remember what I've always told you, all a good-looking woman has to do is put on her lipstick."

Then she sat on the couch and I got her a good hot cup of strong switchel, as she called a satisfactory cup of tea.

I listened as she went into a discourse about her wake. There was no point in being upset about the conversation. She was enjoying it enormously. One by one she went through the people who would attend. She interjected little character titbits about each one, and soon had both of us in stitches.

"So and so will reach out her gannet (birdlike) claw and touch my hair 'Poor Dot!' she'll say, 'Doesn't she look lovely. They did a wonderful job on her, didn't they?'"

I laughed so hard, as she went through her vignettes, that I began to cry.

"Put my crucifix on the wall between the two windows over the casket. That will look lovely, won't it? Make sure you have enough seats for everybody and get as much rest as you can. Wakes can be exhausting, you know, all those people tramping through your house. Thank God, they usually bring food. At least you won't beat yourself to a snot cooking for them. I hope it doesn't happen in the winter, because there's nothing worse than having people tripping over wet boots slung all over the front hall.

"I suppose we won't have any control over when it happens, though. Oh well, my child, do the best you can. That's all anyone can expect.

"Now remember! Don't you dare make me laugh when I'm dying. If you do, I'll haunt you!"

The idea of her haunting me was enough to make me swear on my soul that not only would I never make her laugh, I would not even crack a smile myself. She took me at my word, and that was the end of the subject.

I just knew that someone of my emotional makeup would not respond well to a haunting.

* * * * *

When I finished my commercial course at night school, my mother suggested that I get a part-time job for about three days a week. She made arrangements with my aunt in St. Mary's to have my cousin Barbara come to town and help out with the house.

So it was that I took a job for three days a week at the London, New York and Paris.

It was owned and operated by an impressive man who, I later found out, ran an extremely tight ship. I worked in the ladies department selling gloves, scarves and other small goods.

The store was divided into two sections on the ground floor, with stairs going up to the offices and whatever else was on that upper level. The owner liked to come down the stairs to the landing and stand there watching the action in both sections of the store. He had a fine advantageous view of everything that was going on.

I liked to sneak the odd glance in his direction as he stood there surveying his kingdom. He was a very handsome man with snowy hair, and he always sported a lovely tan. He could be counted on to be impeccably dressed, always in the most stylish of suits.

Although he was not aware of it, I had a connection with his family. The connection was not genetic. I had worn his daughter's hand-me-downs when I was a little girl. My aunt had worked at his home as a servant for a while. I particularly remember a pair of white fur-topped boots and matching white muff.

Upon receiving the finery, my mother must have said, "That's too good for her!" because I've been told by my aunt that I went around decked out in it, telling any and all who would listen, "Dis is too good per me!"

That example of poor self-image must have been one of my first mistakes. I sure don't feel that way anymore, although I still love looking in all the corners of a good second-hand store.

Back at the London, as it was called by everyone in St. John's, there was a sweet little girl from out of town. Her name was Rose; she was very quiet and soft-spoken, with a lovely personality.

The handsome owner of the store did not impress her at all with his good looks. Instead, his very demeanour frightened the life out of her. His mid-morning appearance on the landing was enough to send the blood rushing into her face. It was not a matter of blushing, but of pure, undiluted fear. She was a tiny girl and did her best to hide behind me whenever he made his appearance to check out the activity in his kingdom.

"Oh my God! May he go up and never come down again!"

Every time he appeared she made the same fervent comment, and I had to grab control of myself to keep from bursting out laughing. We worked at glass counters filled with gloves, scarves, underwear and a lot of other stuff. The counters had a glass shelf in the centre, which meant that there were two shelves for us to tidy and keep looking sharp and neat.

Whenever the boss appeared, Rose, after realizing that

I didn't provide sufficient cover, dropped to her knees and began to rearrange the merchandise on both shelves. She somehow managed to stay there until he turned and went back up to where she felt he should have stayed.

"Thank God, he's gone back up!" She'd bounce back to being her normal, happy self. I don't remember seeing such a transformation in a person before or since.

Chapter 33

I don't know just how long I stayed at the store, but I decided to take the Federal Civil Service exam. I passed and was placed on an eligibility list. I was number four on the list, so there were three others before me to be placed in jobs.

In the meantime, after a short stint, I left the London and took some government casual work. One job was at the Census Bureau, and the other was with the Unemployment Insurance Bureau. My mother watched in amazement. I'm sure she didn't think I had brains enough to work for the government. I guess she didn't do any permanent damage by banging my head on the wall, after all.

I don't know if she was relieved, but I sure was.

For recreation I went to the Catholic Youth Club just about every night and danced my feet off. Dances were also held at the St. John's Memorial Stadium. About twice a year Water Street was closed off, and street dances were held there as well. There was no booze sold at the Youth Club, only soft drinks.

A priest was in attendance every night. He usually dropped in and out. One of the regulars handled the music, and he made really great selections. The floor was generally hopping. My brother Lew went there, so Mom had no objections to me going there as well.

Lew was just beginning to become known with that beautiful golden baritone voice. There were concerts, television appearances, radio shows and write-ups in the daily papers. I basked in the reflected fame of this brother of mine. When guys found out he was my brother, they treated me with the utmost respect. No passes at all.

Mom and I watched him on TV and listened to him on the radio. I couldn't help but think how enormously proud of him our father would have been. His talent had been recognized early by our father when he gave the young Lew a few coins to sing for his cronies.

One night Lew came home talking about a new girl he had just met that night. She was an elevator operator at one of the Water Street stores. This was before I joined the Youth Club. That's where he met her, and he was quite smitten at the time.

I told Helen about the budding romance. After a short discussion of the pros and cons of such a move, we decided to take a foray downtown to size her up personally. This would have to be done without my brother's knowledge, of course. He would not have been impressed at all by his nosy little sister, but what the hell! I thrived on danger, and my curiosity was insatiable. Helen was infected by my enthusiasm and happily went along for the ride.

We walked down New Gower Street past all the taverns, simply because we weren't supposed to go down there. We turned down Adelaide Street and headed down the main drag, finally arriving at the store. Trying to look like legitimate shoppers, we headed to the back of the store toward the elevator. I pressed the button and we stood expectantly, waiting for the doors to open. When the elevator finally arrived, Lew's girl stood there in her uniform, staring at us, particularly at me. She had long dark hair and big, brown eyes. She was cute but really nothing to rave about, as far as I was concerned. I could not conceive of her as a future sister-in-law. Not one of my intuition bells even gave a slight jingle.

We disembarked at one of the floors and wandered

around for a while. Finally, without a cent in our pockets and therefore no shopping bags, we found ourselves again pressing the elevator button.

She stared intently at me as the elevator descended. Finally, when we reached the ground floor, she spoke.

"Excuse me? Are you Lew Murphy's sister? You look so much like him!"

"My God," I said to myself, "my cover is blown! That reflected fame of his is pretty powerful stuff!"

I confessed that I was indeed my brother's sister, and she smiled sweetly as the elevator was called upstairs.

Just before the doors closed, I leaned forward. "I'm prettier than he is, though!"

Helen said, "My God, girl! You got a nerve like a bloody toothache! What about if he finds out?"

"So what?" I retorted. "It's a free county! We went into an elevator and she recognized me. That's not my fault, is it? Nah! Besides, how is he going to find out? My lips are sealed, and so are yours. Right?"

If I must say so myself, it was a fine piece of detective work and very satisfying to my ego.

She was not destined to marry my brother, although they did wind up getting engaged. So my intuition was right on target.

She got hooked up with a Yank while my brother was on active duty in Korea, and she sent him a "Dear John" letter.

She left him for a Yank! The kiss of death! He never forgave her, even though she came looking for him at various stages.

Ah! Fame!

Reflected or not, it was a fine thing, and so is intuition. Mine was always right on target, scary sometimes.

My self-esteem went up at least half of a badly needed notch.

* * * * *

Besides being busy at night dancing my feet off at the Catholic Youth Club, I was also busy practising our numbers with the Glee Club. Eventually we were deemed ready to be taken on the road – for concerts to nearby outports.

We went over to Bell Island on the ferry and put on a concert. There was usually a scoff after the concert and a dance following the food. The Lancers was a favourite dance, and we all loved twisting and turning during the vigorous moves.

The local people billeted us and always gave us great breakfasts.

I remember one little town we performed in – the name escapes me now – but it was very picturesque, right on the water. The concert was held in the church hall and, of course, my brother's solo numbers were a resounding success, as usual.

I slept in a feather bed after that concert. I had never experienced such comfort in my life. It was a far cry from my poor folding cot. I even had room in the bed for my feet. What a novel idea.

At the dance after the concert I had been introduced to a young man who was collecting unemployment insurance. When I heard his name, I remembered seeing it on one of the warrants I signed. He also recognized my name from the signature on the cheque.

Anyway, I talked myself out of that potentially embarrassing situation, and he and I had a dance together. He held me uncomfortably close and kept pressing certain parts of his body against relevant parts of mine. For a while there he reminded me of a pretzel; that guy could really contort. He must have thought I was rich, signing all those government cheques.

I got rid of him in short order. My passion did not rise to meet his, thank God.

After we got back to St. John's, I didn't give him another thought. However, later in the workweek I really had no choice but to think of him. As a matter of fact, I had to see him. He turned up at the UIC office asking to see Miss Murphy. My boss looked at me with a question in his eyes as I scurried over to the counter.

My would-be lover stood on the other side of the counter, holding a box of Pot of Gold chocolates, my weakness. I was racking my brain, wondering how the hell I could get rid of him but not the chocolates. I definitely did not want to encourage him in any way, shape or form, but I also didn't want to leave the chocolates behind.

He gave me a sickly smile when he saw me approaching. As I reached the counter he blurted out, "Miss Murphy, you're so beautiful! Will you go to a movie with me tonight?"

Beautiful? I certainly had never thought of myself as being beautiful; my mother, in fact, had reinforced the exact opposite feelings in me. So I was not blown away by his flattery: I just plain did not believe him.

He then informed me that he had come in person to pick up his cheque to take the opportunity to see me again and save the government some stamp money.

"Every penny counts these days, you know, Miss Murphy."

I said to myself, buddy, you're a fine piece of work, that's what you are.

By this time, I had the box of Pot of Gold safely in my hands. I was still wondering how to get rid of him when a brilliant thought streaked through my head.

"I'm so sorry, but my husband would not like this at all. He's very jealous, and he definitely would not babysit our ten-month-old while I took in a movie with another man. He has a frightful bad temper. Why, he gave me a black eye about three weeks ago for no reason at all!"

I clutched the chocolates to my chest. My erstwhile suitor's face turned blood red and his eyes shifted all over the place. He looked everywhere but at me.

I turned nervously, looking at my boss. "Well, thank you so much for the chocolates and for thinking about me, but I really do have to get back to work. You wouldn't want me to get fired would you? My husband would kill me for sure, then. You'd be reading about me in the paper, so you would!"

"By the way," I said, lowering my voice, "it would really be better if you didn't come in to pick up your cheque. The office prefers using the post for delivery. Well, bye-bye now!"

I gave him a cheerful wave as he turned away, and watched as he walked dejectedly out the door and out of my life, thank God. Fame can be a terrible thing, I said to myself as I hurried back to my desk with the chocolates.

My boss nodded toward the counter. "Was that business, Miss Murphy?" he asked, eyeing the chocolates. I nodded yes, it was business and sat at my desk shuffling paperwork and humming.

The boss turned away and walked toward his desk at the end of the room.

He shouted, loud enough for all of us to hear.

"Oh, and Miss Murphy? Cut the racket!"

Crotchety old bugger! I thought to myself. He doesn't have an ounce of romance in his dried-up old soul. Fuck him!

As I was doing some filing, I stuffed a chocolate into my mouth. I would have sworn the taste was close to orgasmic, except I had no clue what an orgasm felt like at that point in my life.

* * * * *

Some strange characters came to the Unemployment Insurance office in my time!

There were also a number of characters who frequented the Catholic Youth Club. Some of them were referred to as "old-timers," meaning they had been around since the club opened, and they attended each and every night of the week.

One of them, Ed, took quite a shine to me and felt it was

his duty to take me under his wing and to warn me about some of the guys floating around the edges of the dance floor.

Ed always came up to me gallantly and bowed from the waist before asking for a dance.

"May I have the honour of dragging your frame around the floor for a scuff?"

I always accepted because I found him very entertaining, and besides, he had told me he liked my intellect. In spite of my mother's disparaging comments about my lack of brains, I was proud of my intellect. I was glad that someone appreciated it. Nobody at home figured I even had a brain, certainly not a functioning one, anyway.

Ed kept up a running commentary as we scuffed around the floor. He'd point every now and then to a tall handsome lady-killer in the crowd and give me the lowdown.

"Now! You see that guy there? If he asks you to dance, for Christ's sake turn him down. He's one of the biggest rams in St. John's. My God! That fellow would rape a rock pile if he thought there was a snake under it! He's not for you, not your type at all. I've seen 'em come and I've seen 'em go! You're a nice girl. Don't let one of those creeps get into your pants! That's all they're looking for, you know. When they're ready to settle down, they'll be looking for a girl whose parents have money. You and I know that your family doesn't have any, so they'd be after you for one thing and one thing only."

After those sage words he escorted me back to my seat and took off, not to return for the rest of the night. He was a good guy and I appreciated his wisdom and knowledge, but I didn't have to worry about the rams. They never asked me to dance, anyway.

My brother, the one with the golden voice, was usually there on the dance floor, too, and he was six foot three, a formidable guy.

The rams were lovers, not fighters. They knew better than to try to pick off the Murphy girl. She had three big brothers – all spoiling for a fight. After all, that's why my brothers carried brass knuckles.

There was a really sweet guy who danced with me regularly. He had just returned from a stint in the air force, and he was the best dancer in the room. He taught me to jive, and I absolutely loved it. His name was Fred, and he often took me home. He had a red station wagon, and we sat in it for a few hours outside my house. We talked about this, that, and anything at all. We laughed ourselves silly, but we never got around to kissing. I was green as grass in those days, and I think he knew it. Come to think about it, he must have been a little green as well.

I met another guy at the Youth Club who was from Corner Brook. He took me on what I felt was a very unusual date. He asked me if I'd like to go to a wrestling match down at the stadium.

I didn't have the slightest interest in wrestling. All I had seen of it was on TV.

My stepfather, bald dome gleaming in the reflected light from the TV screen, straddled his chair and leaned on the back rest to watch wrestling. He dodged imaginary blows, scraping the chair across the floor until I thought he was having a seizure.

Suffice to say I was turned from wrestling. But still, the guy who asked me to go was sort of cute.

He told me that some fellow called "Sky High Low" was to appear at the stadium the night of the match and that he was a really good wrestler. So I said yes, figuring that, at the very least, it would be a new experience.

As a matter of fact, it was the first and last wrestling match I ever attended.

Everywhere I looked the ring seemed to be exploding with acrobatic men, small, big and in between. It was the phoniest, most boring event I had seen in my life. My companion was enjoying it immensely, dodging blows, taking falls and jumping up and down with the rest of the audience whenever something "exciting" happened. There were collective groans, in which he joined, as the crowd showed their displeasure at a particular move by one of the wrestlers. If the place hadn't been so noisy, I'm sure I would have dozed off.

Since I didn't share his passion for wrestling, my young suitor lost interest in me and I never saw him again.

Good riddance, I thought to myself. You get to kiss a lot of frogs before you find a prince.

I was certain I would never recognize the elusive prince when – and if – he ever turned up, so frogs it would have to be. I was ready and waiting for the next one.

Chapter 34

Actually, all the guys in my life were not frogs. There was a prince, although I never did speak to him. I saw him at the library and at Mass on Sundays. He was the most gorgeous-looking guy I had ever seen in my life, and I had the most amazing crush on him. He was tall and blond, and he had a fine physique.

I went to the library to study, but he was always the main attraction. I sat at his table every time, glancing at him now and again in pure adoration. I'm sure he didn't even notice me, but that didn't stop my crush. The crush lasted about three years, but that's all it ever amounted to. However, he did prove to me that there really were princes out there in the big bad world.

I resigned myself to the fact that I would never get anywhere close to him. I said the same thing about him that I had said as a little girl about the new clothes.

"He's too good per me!"

In the meantime I did meet a nice guy and went out with him for about six months. He was very much the gentleman and didn't make a pass during the entire time I was seeing him. We went to movies, and we went to the stadium for skating and dancing. I felt quite at ease with him, but I was definitely not a romantic type.

One night we were saying good night in the front hall, the same dark place in which my stepfather had chased away my first date with his sweeping.

Jack – that was his name – looked at me strangely and told me flatly that I was a "Mama's girl."

I was a little surprised at the comment but made no reply. I couldn't deny that caring for my mother took up a great deal of my time.

The next thing I knew, he began singing a song that was popular at the time. *"Got along without you before I met you, gonna get along without you now!"*

He didn't have a great singing voice, but his diction was fine. I picked up the hint, but didn't rise to the bait; I just let the message go right over my head.

I never laid eyes on him again. What an ignominious end to what could have been a passionate affair! If I had known a thing about passion, that is . . .

Of course I had his phone number, but I didn't call him and he didn't call me. If I hadn't been so emotionally stunted, I would never have let him get away like that.

Years later, when I saw Nicholas Cage in movies, he reminded me a lot of Jack. (Nicholas Cage kind of turned my crank then; he still does as a matter of fact.)

My mother noticed his absence and said, "What happened to Jack?"

I replied, honestly, "I don't know."

"I never liked him much anyway!" she responded

I thought, but didn't say the words out loud, "That's all right. He didn't like you much, either."

I was not destined to mourn him for too long, anyway. One of the girls at work went to Fort Pepperrell every now and then to dances, and she invited me along. I knew that my brothers would do me grievous harm if they ever found out, but I was getting reckless and decided that I would go anyway.

To get to Pepperrell the girls had to take a bus at Parade Street; the bus was sent by the base. The girls had to arrive and leave by the same bus. Hanky-panky was not encouraged.

The Americans were very aware that St. John's men did not like their girls going to the base for dancing or for anything else. In fact, the local guys, including my brothers, were not at all fond of the Americans.

I had one thing going for me; I was a very good dancer,

thanks to my nights at the Catholic Youth Club. I had a great time that night and arrived safely back at Parade Street on the base bus. Some guys I had seen at the base followed the bus by car and picked up the girls they had been dancing with all night. They took off into the dark. I resolved never to do that. I was emerging from my long fog, but I was definitely not that brave.

I hustled down Long's Hill to the relative safety of Allan Square and went to sleep that night with Elvis's "Blue Suede Shoes" drumming through my head.

My friend Moll had never gone to the Youth Club with me, but when she found out I had been to the base, she was interested. It took her about a month, but she finally caved in to her curiosity and decided to go with me.

By that time my friend and I had a regular group of male friends there, and we sat at the same table every time. In the group there were two guys named Bob. We called them "Tall Bob" and "Short Bob."

I introduced Moll to the people at the table, and in no time at all she was up on her feet and dancing. Moll always did have a way with men. "Tall Bob" was quite taken with her and kept her dancing for a while before she begged off for a washroom visit. I accompanied her, and as soon as we got inside the door she turned to me and announced dramatically, "I'm going to marry him, Moll!" (We used the name interchangeably. I was Moll and she was Moll. People probably thought we were two nuts.)

I've always believed I was destined to go to the base and destined to take Moll with me so that she could meet the man who was later to become her husband. Now she not only has her very own Yank, something we craved in our "hubba hubba" days on Water Street, but she is also a Yank herself. Her life is a far cry from Allan Square. They've been married forty-plus years now and are still going strong.

Shortly after Moll met her Prince Charming, she stopped going to the base, and I soon followed her example. After all, I had done my job of introducing them; mission accomplished. I went back to the Youth Club.

Moll had met her prince, but I was still gamely kissing the frogs.

Actually, I did meet a couple of princes, but they never seemed to work out.

One night I went to a dance at the Stadium. Louis Armstrong was in Newfoundland performing for the American servicemen stationed here, and he gave a performance for the troops.

This gorgeous-looking, dark-haired prince came over and asked me to dance. “Blueberry Hill” was being played, and good old Lew was doing his usual great job on the lyrics.

The prince turned out to be a French Canadian with dark, soulful eyes. He was “too good per me.” I just knew it!

He gazed into my eyes and said; “Your eyes tell lies tonight!”

The dance finished, and he was gone. I hadn’t even had a chance to drop my slipper!

Later in the evening I got a glimpse of him on the dance floor. He was caught up in the rapturous embrace of one of my former schoolmates. She was blonde with a great figure. Her eyes were closed, and she was doing some serious cuddling. I viciously hoped that he would break her heart.

I danced with another guy for the rest of the night and accepted when he offered to walk me home.

We said good night circumspectly at my front door. He was the soul of courtesy.

My mother’s cousin who worked at the Pen told my mother I should not see that guy again. He was an ex-con, and the cousin said he was trouble with a capital T.

He had just happened to be walking up our street that night and felt it was his sacred duty to let me know about the guy’s past and possibly his immediate future.

Give or take a few, I guess there were a number of frogs in my orbit.

I still wonder about the French Canadian’s romantic statement: “Your eyes tell lies tonight.”

In the overall scheme of things, it doesn’t really matter.

Maybe it was just one of his standard lines; I guess I'll never know.

It was, though, one of the most unforgettable lines anyone ever handed me. "Beware of mysterious dark strangers" is not a bad piece of advice for a gullible girl from Allan Square.

To give him his due, though, he was one mighty fine-looking prince.

Chapter 35

By the time I was eighteen and had been working for a few years, it was decreed by my mother, after a cursory consultation with me, that it was about time for me to make my appearance in New York, time to meet my father's relatives.

I prepared for my trip with some apprehension. The only Murphy relative I had heard from in my life was my father's only sister, sweet and attentive Aunt Hann. So I wrote her and told her of my imminent arrival. In her return letter she seemed very happy; she was anxious to meet me.

Some of my father's relatives lived on Lexington Avenue in the Bronx. Right about this time I began getting reports from people who were familiar with New York. The consensus was that the Bronx was a tough place, practically a slum. Sounded a bit like my little corner of Allan Square. I figured if I could handle Allan Square I could handle anything, so I went ahead and bought my ticket.

My mother put in her order. She loved pinstripes and she asked me to get her a red and white pinstriped blouse and a matching red skirt. I told her that I should be able to find these things in New York and she agreed, but privately I despaired of ever finding anything that she would like.

I couldn't believe I was going to meet my father's brothers, his mother, and his sister. I wondered if any of the brothers would look like him. The day I was leaving, I was scared stiff. I had never been on a plane, and I had never been off the island of Newfoundland. New York was a long jump from St. John's. What if they didn't like me? It was entirely possible; there were many days when I felt that my own mother wasn't too fond of me, so why should they be any different?

My brother Jerry and his wife took me to the airport and waited until I boarded the flight.

It seemed as if the plane was in the air for hours, but it finally touched down. There were masses of people in the New York airport. I was sure there were not that many people in all of St. John's, and they all seemed to be rushing straight toward me. I roamed around for what seemed like hours after I collected my luggage. The crowds began to thin out and I was starting to get really nervous.

Finally I spotted a man and two teenaged girls sitting on a bench at the far end of the lounge. My feet were killing me, but I smiled at them hopefully, and the man, who I hoped was Uncle Jerry, got up and walked toward me. He put his arms around me and said, "Shirley? Welcome to New York!" Then he introduced me to his two daughters, my cousins.

They looked Italian, and both were very pretty.

We went outside into the burning heat, and after a good deal of walking, we located my uncle's car. I felt like a fish out of water, a real stranger in the night. To ease the slight tension I was picking up from my relatives, I put on the act that always managed to break up my mother. I started cracking jokes like crazy. My uncle Jerry had a very well-developed sense of humour, and in no time at all, he was laughing like crazy and telling his own jokes.

He worked as a bus driver in New York, and he regaled me with stories of some of the characters he ran into daily. Just as I was starting to enjoy myself, we arrived at his place. He didn't live on Lexington Avenue, but he did live in the Bronx. His wife was Italian and very friendly. She had a meal of spaghetti and meatballs ready. It was the first time I'd ever tasted real Italian food, served with garlic bread, yet. That was another first for me. It was delicious!

Within a fairly short time after my arrival, the phone started to ring. It was the relatives, wondering if the country cousin had arrived safely. He assured them that I was safely on terra firma and enjoying my dinner. I knew that he had been my father's youngest and favourite brother. He still missed him; I could tell by the look in his eyes when he spoke of my dad.

"It was the saddest day of my life when your father got on that boat and returned to Newfoundland. He left his whole family behind to go back. I knew then I was saying goodbye to him forever. Anyway, enough sadness! You didn't come all this distance to be sad. So tell me about your mother and your brothers. What's Newfoundland like now? What's the population of St. John's? I bet it's a lot bigger than when we all lived there!"

He didn't mention my stepfather, and that was fine by me.

He thought I was so funny, a "real pisser," he called me. That meant someone who was a real character. I guess he must have figured I'd be even funnier after a few drinks, so he plied me with vodka and orange juice. The only thing that happened was I slowly got sleepier and more boring, to the point where it was too much trouble getting my tongue around any words at all.

I clammed up completely and started to slide down my chair. They finally showed me to my bedroom, where I promptly got down on the floor, crawled under the bed and went out like a light.

Sleeping under the bed must have been caused by some deep subconscious urge from my childhood, maybe an urge for privacy, maybe the "fight or flee" syndrome. I had been, after all, fighting that one all my life. At least there was no danger of wetting the bed while sleeping under it. Who knows? Maybe that was the reason.

Anyway, I woke up still under the bed the next morning, sick as a dog, nursing a blinding headache. It was enough to make me realize that I was at least one gene short of the Murphy drinking allotment, thank God.

Welcome to New York!

I had been looking forward to having a nice one-on-one chat with Aunt Hann, but the whole time I was there, the opportunity did not arise. She worked every day in a school cafeteria and could not get any time off. She was very warm and affectionate during the times I did get to see her, but no intimate chats.

As a matter of fact, I was very soon handed over to her daughter Mary, and I stayed there for most of my visit. She did not go out to work, and she took me everywhere.

The third day I was in New York, I had a great surprise. My brother Lew, who was stationed with the army in Camp Petawawa, Ontario, came down to New York by bus. I was never so glad to see anyone in my life. He and my uncles went out to little neighbourhood bars and dragged me along to some of them. I was bored out of my tree.

My cousin Mary told me she saw more of New York during my visit than she had in her entire life. She took me to visit St. Patrick's Cathedral, the zoo, the Statue of Liberty; we did all the tourist things. She was a great sport.

We also went to the top of the Empire State Building, where I told her I felt like jumping. She said, "Oh, you have a fear of falling!" I replied that I wasn't exactly scared of falling. It was more like I was scared of jumping. She looked at me strangely, but let my comment pass.

I met my grandmother one night at some relative's apartment. I found her to be very cold and uncommunicative. She probably thought the same about me. There was no kiss or hug volunteered by her, nor by me. We were strangers. It was kind of sad.

All the cousins did their best to entertain me. One night we went in a group to Greenwich Village, where a lot of strange people hung out. One of my cousins warned me to be careful whom I danced with, because the person could be a woman dressed up as a man. I thought we were going to Sodom and Gomorrah.

We went to a strip club that night in the Village, and I really liked that. I've always loved strip music.

Mary and I went shopping a number of times. I picked up a blouse and matching skirt for my mother. To my surprise, when I got home and showed it to her, she loved it. You never know.

All in all it was a good visit, and the cousins were very gracious to someone they had never met before. I did not regret making the trip, but nobody there looked even a little like my dad. I guess that was expecting a bit much.

I don't remember who took me to the airport for the return trip home.

I next saw my uncle Jerry about forty years later. He had moved to Florida, as had my aunt Hann and cousin Mary. My uncle had been mugged in New York, and that did it for them.

I went to Florida with my brother Lew, his treat. He was a great one for treating people to trips. About ten years before our visit to Florida, he had brought our uncle and his wife to St. John's. Uncle Jerry was in the beginning stages of Parkinson's disease, and he was using a walker. It was the first time he had seen St. John's since the whole family had left for the States so many years before. He didn't know anybody there, and the city had changed quite a bit, but they had a great time.

When we went to visit him in Florida, my uncle was in a nursing home. We brought him a big, white teddy bear. He knew us both.

His wife came into the room while we were there, and I saw his brown eyes melt with tenderness. He reached out a shaking hand and grabbed hers. He spoke very softly and romantically.

For a few minutes he reminded me of the uncle I had met on my visit to New York so many years before.

"I still get the old feelings," he said to his wife, "Do you still get the old feelings?" He looked directly into her eyes as he asked the question.

My God! I remember thinking it was so wonderful and so sad.

I brushed away my tears. Sometimes that's all that's left – the old feelings.

Chapter 36

After I went to work full-time, my mother and I rarely fought during the weekdays. There were a few memorable rows, though, especially the one when she used her paralyzed arm as a weapon against me and drew blood. That one was a real shocker.

Mostly the battles were on the weekends – Saturdays, as a matter of fact. I was becoming really battle-weary and seriously thought about moving to a boarding house, but I simply could not do it. She needed me too much, and so I stayed and took it. I could never remember what started any of the fights, but I know that I fought back. I would have had to be dead to offer no resistance.

I had grown up throwing salt over my left shoulder so that a fight wouldn't start. I might as well have thrown the whole shaker, for all the good that did. Crossed knives on the table sent a chill down my back, and I always hurried to straighten them up. That did me a fat lot of good. The shit hit the fan regularly, no matter which way the knives were sitting on the table or how often I refilled the salt shaker.

I didn't even confess to fighting with my mother during the weekly confession sessions. Fighting was such a regular part of my life that I realized confessing it would make absolutely no difference in the overall scheme of things.

One of our biggest rackets was about my mother's hair. I have always been hopeless at doing my own hair; I had no flair at all. My mother used to have a lady who came to the house to do her hair, the proper way she liked it done.

One day, for some reason or other, she asked me to do it for her. My God! My hands were shaking as I stood over her and looked down at the top of her head. I just knew, without a shadow of a doubt, that I couldn't do it to her liking. Sure enough, as I stood fumbling with the rollers and her hair, up she suddenly blew. She grabbed the comb from my hand and told me to get to hell's fiery flames out of her sight – I was useless as a daughter!

The words stung, but I had heard them before, and I knew that I should have been given an A for effort. I was really trying to do my best, while knowing that it would never be good enough.

She threw the rollers and the comb on the floor and shouted at me.

"I hope to Christ that you get a daughter just like you!"

One of her regular complaints against me was that I always had to have the last word. Unable to hide my wounded expression, I retorted, "I should be so lucky!"

I thought she was putting a curse on me that day, but as it turned out, it must have been a blessing.

My daughter, Andrea, is more than any mother could ever want, and she has a wonderful flair with the curling iron. When she fixes my hair, it looks exactly like a professional job. If I had been more like my daughter, my mother would have been satisfied.

When we weren't fighting, my mother and I were laughing. It was a crazy life. She absolutely loved my sense of humour and often commented on how much it was like hers. Talk about confusing!

"God bless that girl's sense of humour!" She made that comment to any and all who would listen.

Moll and I used to pretend we were running a brothel and that Mom was the madam. She nearly rolled out of the bed with laughter. Mom had an earthy sense of humour. As she said, it was just like mine.

Every now and then, when a joke crossed the line, she withdrew her approval and said in a no-nonsense manner:

"Remember now, madam! I am your mother."

My stepfather was never involved in any of our rackets. I guess that most of the time he was out somewhere, playing cards with his friends. He probably had a couple of buddies.

In all the time my mother was married to him, I have to admit he didn't lay a finger on me, nor did he and I have any fights. Luckily, because I had my hands full dealing with my mother's moods, my stepfather joining in the fray would have been just too much for me to handle.

I was always leery of him, though. He lent some validity to my feelings about three weeks before I got married.

As usual, I don't remember what started it. But he came out of my mom's bedroom and, to finish up whatever we had been fighting about, he pushed his shoulder into me and nearly knocked me off my feet. He shouted, with a bitterness that shocked me, "If you cared anything about your mother, you wouldn't be getting married! I fed you!" That one made me see red. I screamed back at him, "You didn't feed me, I worked like a dog for every slice of bread! My brothers fed me!"

What did he expect of me, to stay there and nurse them both into their old age? I was not that type of girl. I wanted a family of my own. I desperately wanted someone to love me. My mother didn't see him shove me that day, and if she had, I'm not at all sure she would have risen to my defence.

Strangely enough, I had met the man I was destined to marry. Where else, but at the Catholic Youth Club?

The second time I saw him, he said, "I'm going to marry you, Murph!"

Then I didn't see him again for four years. He made dates with me, but stood me up. That should have been my number one warning, but as they say, and I'm inclined to believe, love is indeed blind.

Besides, he recited Oscar Wilde's *Ballad of Reading Gaol* to me. That did it for my romantic and love-starved soul. When I first started seeing him, I was unable to say "I'm sorry" or "I love you." Those were phrases that were unacceptable in my family. I had never used the words, nor had the words ever been put to me. I cannot remember anyone ever saying them. Although my father probably had done so when I was small, before he died. I do remember feeling love from him. Maybe that's the way things were done in those days. That's the way they were done in our house, anyway.

My prospective husband had a drinking problem, wouldn't you just know it. You'd think that with my experience with booze I would have recognized the symptoms at the start, but I really didn't.

When I showed my mother my engagement ring with its modest diamond, she looked at it and then at me and said, "I suppose you think you're being smart now!" I was baffled at her reaction, but she kept me in the dark, not elaborating in any way.

One of the things I loved about the man I was to marry was the fact that when he came into my life the loneliness I had felt for as long as I could remember suddenly left, and I felt safe. He always said that he was the only man who had the guts to go into our house and take me out. That might have been true.

The strange thing was that, after my marriage, my mother and I never had another cross word. No more fights. It was lovely. When I said goodbye to her after a visit, she always said, "God love you, my child." I think that was her way of saying "I love you."

It was a wonderful relief to have no more fights. This was the way things should have been between us all those years. I thoroughly enjoyed our new relationship.

A few days after I married, a friend of mine dropped in to see her, and my mother said to her, "Now that Shirley is gone, I have no one to fight with anymore." She actually missed the fighting, but I didn't. Her sharp tongue turned softer, and she was gentler with me. I gradually felt myself relaxing in her presence. The sense of humour, her saving grace, remained sharp, caustic and wholly entertaining. We had some great talks, some great laughs, and our relationship turned into a nurturing one.

The boys no longer seemed to be her only children; I

began to find my own place. I think she finally saw the truth in the old adage, "A son is a son till he takes a wife, but a daughter is a daughter all of her life."

My mother was about to be rescued from the house she had survived in all of her married life. My brother Lew decided to buy the ramshackle place we called home. The absentee landlord was contacted in the States, and he jumped at the chance to sell the old house. The renovations soon began. My mother refused to leave, staying there all the while the work was going on. The only time she gave in to pressure was when her bedroom was being done, and then she came to my place and stayed for two days.

She wound up getting a large bathroom with a lovely bath and a washbasin, something she had long deserved. It was a far cry from the toilet in the dark washroom in the hall; as a matter of fact, that one should not even have been called a washroom because there was no sink.

The new toilet naturally had a lovely toilet seat cover. What a novel and comfortable experience! My mother was finally getting the few small comforts she had so richly deserved all her life. They were long overdue.

One day she said to me, as we were sitting in the unfinished kitchen, "Wouldn't it be funny if, just as this place is finished, I kicked the bucket?"

I shivered at her words.

They turned out to be strangely prophetic.

Chapter 37

While I was busy dodging the verbal darts from my mother's sharp tongue, Helen was kept equally busy trying to stay out of the range of her granny's impressive verbal fusillade.

Helen, Moll and I ran for the hills whenever we saw the window opening in the upstairs flat of number eight. The granny's screams of abuse could be heard as far away as Dick's Square. Helen became very adept at timing her granny's arrival on the steps of our house.

She always managed to get in the door and partway up the stairs before her granny was able to make an appearance.

Every oath that was in the granny's vocabulary was rained down on Helen's head, even when she was in the street playing with her friends. Even Moll and I – who were both accustomed to being sworn at – winced when we heard Helen's granny in all her glory.

Her mother wanted her desperately, but Helen was never allowed to see her. I didn't think that was very fair. Helen and I discussed the whole situation quite frequently. When we were ten or eleven, we decided that the time had come to remedy the injustice. We would go find her mother.

It was, of course, to be a top-secret mission. We got her address from the phone book and decided that we would leave from school on an appointed day and simply turn up at her mother's place. Helen's mother had two other daughters and a son, Helen's half-siblings.

We thought this was very exciting, and Helen was starving for her mother and her sisters and brother.

It was decided that, when we got back home, neither of us would tell the truth about where we had been after school, or why we were late. We had simply gone for a walk, was to be the story.

When the day arrived at last, we walked north on Barnes Road instead of going south to Harvey Road, which was our usual route. We took our time strolling toward the back of St. John's, where Helen's mother lived. When we got there, we asked a boy for directions.

He immediately pointed to the house. We walked over and stared in the window before knocking on the door. We were both shaking. Helen's mother answered the door and, of course, had no difficulty in recognizing her daughter, who would have stood out in a crowd of a hundred girls. I remember her welcome as being very warm – rapturous, as a matter of fact. We were invited into the house and that's the end of my memory, until we found ourselves walking home after the visit.

We were both beginning to feel decidedly nervous by this time. I was more nervous than Helen, because from that day on she always had her mother. I had only one home and nary a soul I could run to for refuge.

My mother, her face frozen in rage and what could have been worry, met me in the hall. Before Helen was able to make it halfway up the stairs, my mother demanded to know where I had been. Following our plan, I lied and told her we had gone for a walk after school. Of course, I neglected to mention the visit Helen and I had paid to her mom.

Helen, for some strange reason, told her granny the truth, the whole truth and nothing but the truth. Her granny promptly came down the stairs and imparted the news to my mother, who gave me the rounds of the kitchen and read me the riot act about lies and my audacity at daring to tell her anything but the truth. I was sent to bed without any supper, to reflect on my sins with an empty stomach.

I woke about three in the morning, starved and worried. I looked at the table beside my bed and saw an apple sitting there. It warmed my soul and helped to fill my belly. Maybe she did love me after all.

That was the last time I went to Helen's mother's place, but it was not the last time for Helen. She visited regularly and got to know the kids and her mother. When Helen was about fourteen, she finally left Allan Square, left our school, and went to live with her mom.

I can't say that I blame her. Her grandmother was an absolutely impossible woman, hard as a rock from a rock-hard life, the poor woman.

Every now and then she came down from upstairs to sit and visit with my mom. She was there for some of our arguments, and she was not shy about joining in the fray, never on my side, of course. I needed her input like a hole in the head; my mother was quite capable of handling things on her own.

"My God, missus!" she'd say to Mom, egging her on. "If you could only see the dirty looks that one is giving you behind your back! I tell you, she'll bate you one of these days! I can see her giving you a good crack across the face in a couple of years. She's a bad little bitch, so she is, the little whore!"

Whore? I beg your pardon, you old biddy! God rest your soul, anyway.

Finally, she got too old to stay in the flat alone, and her daughter came and made arrangements for her to go into a home. She did not go quietly into the good nursing home, though. She fought against the dying of the light, resisting all the way.

My mother and my brother Lew visited her every Sunday. I think the nursing home was in the Goulds. When they visited they brought her Pepsi, raisin squares and some boiled ham for a little treat.

Every now and then she managed to run away from the home and somehow or other made it back to Allan Square, where she collapsed in a ball of clothing on the floor and begged my mother not to let them take her back. She vowed that she would not be any trouble and that she would sleep on the floor in a corner, if only she could stay. The poor old lady became hysterical at the thought of going back.

But the police always arrived and gently took her back to the home. They were very kind, but it was still terribly sad, and I did feel sorry for her. After all, she was a product of her environment, which I understood had not been a great one.

All these years later I can still see the strange scene of Helen and her aged grandparents slowly making their way up the stairs of our house. I had no idea that they would be moving in that day. It was just before my father passed away.

It was a tableau set in stark tones of black and white: The little old lady with her snow-white hair and long, black coat, laboriously making her way up the stairs, followed by the beautiful little girl and her short black coat, and the tall old gentleman, black overcoat trailing the steps, and his white hair gleaming, bringing up the rear.

The only spark of colour in the scene was the flame in Helen's red curls. It was as if God had sent me a beautiful sister. She was my age, and she would live at Allan's Square for only seven years.

Although we didn't know it, there was someone just aching to tell Helen that he loved her. My brother Bob, who was two years younger than we were, had a heart just bursting with love for my fiery-haired little friend.

He even took to visiting her granny and sitting upstairs waiting for Helen to come home, so that he could feast his eyes on the love of his young life. For some reason or other, he thought the old lady was Helen's mother.

I learned later that he shadowed us practically every day and knew exactly where Helen, Moll and I were just about every hour. He should have been a private eye. We didn't have a clue that we were being followed. God alone knows what he might have seen, surmised or imagined, the little snot!

Chapter 38

With the verbal abuse I endured at home, naturally, I didn't have a very good self-image. I did well in school, was accomplished in writing poetry, was a member of the Glee Club, and sang with the senior girls' choir at the nine o'clock Mass every Sunday morning, but nothing really seemed to impress my mother.

I found great comfort in keeping the house clean and in preparing the meals when my mother was under the weather. She was fairly compliant when she was feeling too miserable to care about what was being done and how it was being done.

But when she arose from her bed like Lazarus from the tomb, the atmosphere changed swiftly from an uneasy quiet to open warfare once again. Everything I had done while she was sick immediately went under the microscope and was pulled to pieces and tossed aside.

Strangely enough, while I was kissing all those frogs, and my stepfather was industriously sweeping the remainders out our front door, I had unknowingly met the man who was destined to become my first husband and the father of my children.

The gossip at the Youth Club was that my reluctant love enjoyed drowning in his cups. That could have accounted for his mysterious disappearances.

So I ignored the man who would be my first love. I moved on – to my very own Yank.

The only hitch was that the Yank had been married and

was separated. When I told my mother of his marital status, she nearly spit up her tea.

"Bullshit!' she choked out. "Only eggs are separated, you silly little bitch!"

I loved it when she used endearments.

All good things must come to an end, and sure enough, the time came for my very own Yank to make his way back to the States. Moll was still entertaining hers in their front room across the street. I said a fond farewell to him and his land of milk and honey.

I decided to enter the convent; might as well offer my virginity where it would be appreciated, was the way I figured it.

Besides, anything would have been better than remaining in the house on Allan Square.

My mother watched as I changed my brother's first child and announced, "You'll never enter the convent, my child. You were born to be a mother!"

Her observation must have had something to do with the way I held the tube of diaper-rash cream. I don't recall feeling any maternal emotions at that time.

In the meantime, while waiting to give up worldly pleasures and donning the habit for the remainder of my natural life, I found myself longing for a dance.

I reminded myself a bit of Scarlett O'Hara in her widow's weeds, when the formidable Captain Rhett Butler claimed her and whirled her onto the dance floor.

I decided to go to a dance that was being held on Water Street. In deference to my convent leanings, I chose to wear a black sheath that I had bought during my visit to New York.

There he was, this cute guy, standing next to me and staring up a storm.

"John?"

"Murph?" He wasn't sure who I was, but I knew him. We danced together the rest of the night, and we soon discovered that the old magic was still alive and kicking.

He vetoed the convent idea right away and announced once again that he was going to marry me. Soon!

For some strange reason, this new suitor skipped being confined to the outer reaches of the front hall like all the others. He was welcomed into the front room right off the bat.

My brother Bob, who was rarely around the house at all, suddenly developed a real fondness for the front room, and he joined us there regularly. When Bob showed no signs of leaving, he was given the price of an order of fish and chips, after which he happily left us alone.

Which left my suitor free to pursue defrosting his soon-to-be virgin bride.

He deserved the comfort of the couch. And I liked it, too.

We met at the Water Street dance in September, and we were married the following February.

He seemed to have mended his ways as far as drinking was concerned. I didn't see him tipsy until the night of our wedding. As one of my brothers put it, "He's only stopping until he gets you!"

The mother of my soon-to-be husband insisted that I was years older than he was, because of my greying hair. He was actually two years older than I, but I didn't argue with her.

My mother nodded her head sagely and uttered profound words. "Marry in haste and repent at leisure."

I recognized that hers was the voice of experience, and her prophetic tone made me feel vaguely uneasy.

Chapter 39

The wedding date was changed from January to February; the reason for the change escapes me now. Maybe I needed a little more time to plan things or to adjust to the fact that I would be leaving Allan Square.

It didn't take very long to choose my wedding dress and veil. I simply dropped into the London one day after work and found the dress almost right away. It was not a full-length one; that would not have been the thing for a winter wedding. I put it on layaway in November and paid it off.

Getting something for my mother to wear was not nearly so simple. She was not easy to please, and she could not get out to do her own shopping. I understood her frustration.

So I scouted the stores on Water Street and selected one or two dresses each time that she might be able to tolerate; I took them on approval. But she did not approve. Mom didn't like anything I brought home. My nerves were getting frayed, and my patience was wearing thin.

To make matters worse, my soon-to-be husband passed me fifty dollars and suggested that I drop into the jewellery store across from my office on Duckworth Street. He honestly didn't see any sense in both of us choosing the wedding band, and, jellyfish that I was, I let him get away with that one. Six months after the wedding, the ring turned my finger green. I remember wondering if maybe that was an omen.

Mom and I gave up trying to get her a ready-made dress from any of the stores. Instead, we went through her scanty wardrobe and found nothing suitable. Finally, she had the brilliant idea of wearing one of my dresses. I had a beautiful red-velvet princess dress. She decided to try it, and, surprise of surprises, it fit her to a "T"! This was after a month of bringing home dresses for approval. I heaved a sigh of relief, and she seemed reasonably contented.

The girls at work had a shower for me, and then Mom's sister had one at her place.

After those details were taken care of, there was nothing but to wait for the fateful night and the breaching of the maidenhead.

I didn't have an ounce of passion running through my veins. My emotional growth was definitely stunted. I kept remembering my mother's words, that a woman was nothing more than a waste receptacle for a man during intercourse. I didn't envy my soon-to-be husband. Was he going to be turned off? Talk about getting a pig in a poke!

I was sure the "deflowering" would be horrific. I bought myself a pair of hot-pink babydoll pyjamas to see if they would make me feel at least a touch warm; maybe hot was too much to expect from a girl who could not go to sleep at night before saying an Act of Contrition.

Not only that, I absolutely hated the way he kissed. Bad sign. He slobbered all over my face and literally poured his spittle into my mouth. Granted, I had been emotionally starved all of my life, but I had never really known thirst. This unexpected bathing of my face and force-feeding of fluids was definitely too much for any self-respecting virgin to endure.

From the advantage of my advanced years, I can honestly say I really didn't feel that virginity is the best preparation for marriage. Oops! Act of Contrition called for tonight, definitely.

Still, I was not expecting my hot-pink babydolls to send him mad with red-hot passion. I decided to wait and see.

You never really know. Just because I didn't appeal to myself naked didn't mean that I wouldn't appeal to him.

I decided, the night before my wedding, that I would not sleep in my ice-cold bedroom. Instead, I grabbed my pillow and blanket and slept on the daybed in the kitchen. It was toasty warm in front of the big oil stove.

I turned on the radio very low and snuggled down in the daybed.

My mind raced from thought to thought as I waited for sleep to come. I thought a lot about my dad. Behind my closed eyes I could feel the kitchen transforming into the happy place it used to be before his death. The spoons were being played, with the accordion and the mouth organ. It all melded in nicely with the music from the radio. I saw myself as a little girl dancing on my father's shoes to the strains of "Black Velvet Band."

Round and round the floor we went, swept up in the joy of the music.

Then, in the dream, I heard my mother screaming at him, "Have you been drinking McMannis's piss again?"

McMannis was his favourite bootlegger. I realized, for the first time, that neither of my mother's marriages had been a bed of roses. Those were hard, hard times. I did know for sure that my father was her first love. I felt happier.

The day of my wedding dawned dark and dreary. Moll, of course, was my maid of honour. She arrived at the front door about seven o'clock, already arrayed in her blue dress. She looked simply lovely.

Before I could begin to get ready for the nine-thirty ceremony, I had to make my mother's breakfast. The lumpy Cream of Wheat with some toast and tea were soon placed before her in bed. She gamely refrained from commenting on the Cream of Wheat and left only the toughest and most obvious of the lumps.

The wedding was taking place in the Marian Chapel at the Basilica. That meant a lot of walking for my mother, who had been crippled after her stroke. But with my help she finally made it. She did not complain. She and I were getting along much better since my wedding had been announced. I like to think she realized finally that I wasn't such a bad daughter after all.

The people I cared about were waiting in the chapel. Mom's sister, my favourite aunt, was there with her husband. My brothers were there, and at the front of the chapel, the man himself. He looked mighty fine in a new brown suit with dark stripes.

During the Mass my brother Lew sang the *Ave Maria* in his beautiful baritone, and it was so moving that it nearly transported me right up onto the altar. People usually paid him to sing at their weddings, but he did it for free at mine.

I have absolutely no memory of the wedding ceremony. If I was "given away" by some male member of my family, I also cannot remember that. Maybe nobody gave me away; maybe they simply gave thanks that I was finally going.

Mom had twisted my stepfather's arm and he'd agreed to spring for a wedding breakfast at a downtown restaurant. So we all headed there after the ceremony. I don't have a clue what we ate. There was no wedding cake. My mother said, "Whoever heard of cake with breakfast? You don't need a cake. Don't push your luck."

My husband and I had arranged to go for dinner at the Balsam Hotel on Barnes Road. We also had a room booked for the night. I had not seen him drink before; I had only heard tales of his excesses. He started to drink right after the wedding breakfast. I was not impressed.

I was very leery of drinking men, owing to childhood trauma.

Anyway, we all headed back to Allan Square so that I could change. Moll was in fine fettle. She also liked to take a drink, and she was becoming extremely happy in her cups.

Moll cornered my new husband and warned him, "You be good to her, you son of a bitch!"

My mother suddenly called for quiet. She held up her cup of tea and sized up everyone before resting her eyes on me. "A son is a son till he takes a wife, but a daughter's a daughter all of her life!"

I had my coat on by this time, and we were ready to leave. I hadn't kissed her since the day about ten years before, when she had told me not to bother. But she stood there and looked at me. "Aren't you going to kiss me goodbye?" I did.

I heard later that, after I left the house, Mom cut off the booze, pointed to Moll and said to my brother Lew, "Get her the hell out of here! Now."

My new husband and I were headed for Barnes Road and the lovely old Balsam Hotel.

We had a beautiful dinner in the quaintly appointed dining room and then headed upstairs to our room.

By this time, it was nearing eight o'clock.

Before I realized what was happening, a bottle of booze and a flask mysteriously appeared from his overcoat pocket. I could almost hear him thinking, "Hot time in the old town tonight!"

Maybe he needed some Dutch courage, poor bugger.

Anyway, when I eventually came out of the bathroom, bedecked in my hot-pink babydolls and perfumed like a Halifax whore, he was waiting for me, naked as a jaybird, obviously fortified by some of his liquor and ready for action.

Although I had grown up in a houseful of men, I had never before laid eyes on a naked one. My new husband did appear to have some degree of modesty. His hand was carefully placed over his package, as if to shield it from my virgin eyes, poor bastard. God, were we both fucked up!

It was, however, the nineteen fifties. Between the nuns and my mother, I was the warped product of a very strange upbringing.

That's not an excuse, but it could loosely be called a reason for my inhibitions. I have no insights into his particular hang-ups.

He quickly downed a full drink, for courage, I presumed. Maybe he used a straw, that's how quickly the glass emptied. Then he began weaving his way toward me. I suddenly realized that my new husband was well on his way to becoming blitzed.

The next thought in my mind was, *When does the fighting start?*

Anyway, between the jigs and the reels, I managed to elude him, flopping on the bed in a futile attempt to adopt a provocative pose and to live up to the promise of my perfume, "Evening in Paris."

I think by this time he was still sober enough to be disappointed; he expected me to be naked. He showed no appreciation for my babydolls. I felt deeply wounded.

He reached the foot of the bed, dropped all pretence of false modesty, and made a flying leap at me that was worthy of a seasoned circus performer. It knocked the wind right out of my sails and I gasped for air.

Sweet Jesus! I thought to myself, *What have I done?*

The next things to go were the babydolls. I found them the next morning under the bed.

I didn't have to worry about being drowned by his spittle. There were no kisses, no endearments, simply "Wham! Bam!"

Not even a "Thank you, ma'am." He simply rolled over and went out like a light.

He resurfaced periodically during the night for another drink, and the same process was repeated, time after time. I had to hand it to him, he had definite staying power, as long as he could get the odd nap to rebuild his strength and the odd drink to renew his courage.

Either that or the "Evening in Paris" was working overtime.

Toward the end of that long and exhausting night, he stirred and rolled over once more, but this time he didn't reach for me.

Instead, he threw up the precious booze he had imbibed during the evening, all over the bed, the floor, his pillow. I jumped from the bed to the floor, narrowly escaping being hit with the flying fluid.

I raced into the bathroom and was violently sick. What an unforgettable wedding night.

From that time on, there was an integral part of myself that I kept hidden from him. It was my secret holdback. I loved him many times during the twenty-one years we spent together, but I was never again *in* love with him.

The little part of me that was kept inviolate was the part that enabled me to fall in love again later in life.

Afterword

The defining event in my life was my father's death, but for as long as I can remember, I have dreamed of him only once.

In the only dream I ever had of my father, I saw myself as an adult woman, walking up Allan Square. The atmosphere in the square had changed. It was totally quiet. No sign of life at all. There were no yelling children, no chatting mothers, no slamming front doors, no barking dogs.

The old house, however, was exactly as it had been when we lived there: ramshackle, wind-battered and poor. Inside, it was entirely a different story. I had never seen the place look so bright. I wandered through the rooms in a daze. Each of the beds was covered with brightly patterned homemade quilts. Somehow I knew they had been made by Mom's mother, our Nanny Kelly in Tickle Cove. The walls were alive with floral wallpaper.

I stopped in the lobby and lifted the latch of the coal pound door. It was empty and a chill seemed to ooze from the walls of the place. I quietly closed the door and walked through the kitchen to the half-door leading to the backyard.

My mother and father were there, looking young and happy. I could not recall ever having seen them that young.

My four brothers were racing around, wild and free as only little boys can be.

A little girl with long, dark hair was sitting on a bench cradling a baby doll. I recognized her immediately, and she looked deeply into my eyes. Then she got up, still carrying her baby doll, and walked to my side. She put her hand in mine, and I could feel her trust and love pouring over me.

I turned around to face my mother and father, and I noticed that my dad held a white envelope in his hand. He opened the envelope and withdrew an old black key. I recognized it as the one that was used for the front door of the house on Allan Square.

I stared into his beautiful brown eyes and said, "I'm taking her with me."

He nodded, handed me the key and looked down with tenderness at the little girl clinging to my hand.

He said, "You come back whenever you want to."

So I have listened to his words and have gone back, even to the infamous coal pound.

And I have taken her out.

The End

Acknowledgements

Thanks to my eldest son, Tim Breen, for his sound editorial and technical advice. He led me into the "Coal Pound" and brought me out again. He listened to all my stories.

Thank you to my son Kent Breen who worked like a dog, bringing the old family photos back to life.

The picture on the front cover of Allan Square is Kent's work.

My son Mark Breen and my daughter, Andrea Scott, were solidly in my corner, cheering me on all the way. Thanks guys.

My nephew Noel Murphy hunted for pictures in St. John's. The shot of the bandstand in Bannerman Park is Noel's work, also the shots of modern-day Allan Square and the Kirk.

Michelle Stewart has been a wonderful friend of laughter and fun since we first met. I consider her one of my life's many blessings.

Thanks to Susan Rendell, my editor at Flanker, for her eagle eye and great personality.

Peter Hanes, my "Middle Man" at Flanker, is a saint in his own right, with great patience and humour.

Thank you to Garry Cranford, publisher of Flanker Press, and Margo and Jerry Cranford for their copyediting.

About the Author

Shirley Murphy had always thought she was born on Allan Square. Throughout the writing of this memoir, at the age of seventy-one, she finally discovered she was actually born December 23, 1936, on Livingstone Street. Her family moved to Allan Square when she was a year old.

She moved out of the neighbourhood when she married at the age of twenty-three. Her three sons, Tim, Mark and Kent, were born in 1960, 1961, and 1962. Shirley's brother Jack promptly dubbed her "Pregnancia." In 1965 her young family moved to Ontario. Shirley's only daughter, Andrea, was born there in 1967.

Shirley was a stay-at-home wife and mother. Drawing inspiration from the antics of her four children and their friends, she wrote weekly columns for various newspapers, including, among others, the original Toronto *Sunday Sun*.

"Forced put being no man's choice," she went back to school at the age of forty-three to prepare herself for re-entering the workforce.

Shirley Murphy lives in Bowmanville, Ontario, with her second husband, Ron. Between them they have nine children.